THE
STRANGEST
OF STRANGE

UNSOLVED
MYSTERIES
VOLUME 1

**Books by Phyllis Raybin Emert
from Starscape Books**

The Strangest of Strange Unsolved Mysteries, Volume 1
The Strangest of Strange Unsolved Mysteries, Volume 2

THE STRANGEST OF STRANGE

UNSOLVED MYSTERIES

VOLUME 1

PHYLLIS RAYBIN EMERT

STARSCAPE

THE STRANGEST OF STRANGE UNSOLVED MYSTERIES, VOLUME 1

Previously published as *Mysteries of Lost and Hidden Treasure*, copyright © 1996 by RGA Publishing Group, Inc. *Ghosts, Hauntings and Mysterious Happenings*, copyright © 1992 by RGA Publishing Group, Inc.

Interior art by Jael

A Starscape Book
Published by Tom Doherty Associates, LLC
175 Fifth Avenue
New York, NY 10010

www.tor-forge.com

ISBN 978-0-7653-6595-8

First Starscape Edition: October 2010

Printed in August 2010 in the United States of America by Offset Paperback Manufacturers in Dallas, Pennsylvania.

0 9 8 7 6 5 4 3 2 1

For Ron and Cora Raybin,
and Joshua Benjamin Emert

Contents

GHOSTS, HAUNTINGS, AND MYSTERIOUS HAPPENINGS

MYSTERIES OF LOST and HIDDEN TREASURE

Here Today,
Gone Tomorrow

The telegraph cable stretched across the sandy bottom of the ocean floor like a huge serpent. There had been a break in the line, and a diver was sent down into the depths near Palm Beach, Florida, to find the problem and repair it. Wasting little time, the diver began carefully to check the entire length of the cable, searching for the break or disturbance in the line.

The name of the diver is not known, nor is the exact date of this incident. It probably took place early in the twentieth century, after the first Atlantic telegraph cable was laid (1866) and soon after Palm Beach became an incorporated city (1911), but likely before wireless long-distance radio communication became routine (late 1920s).

Suddenly, out of the corner of his eye, the diver became aware of a large dark mass. His mind flashed an immediate danger signal to his body, and he froze instantly.

"Shark?" he thought as he focused on the dark shape to the side and ahead of him. After a nervous few moments, the diver realized the mass wasn't moving, and he began to relax. But his curiosity had been aroused.

He swam closer and discovered, much to his surprise, the wreck of an ancient ship half buried in the sand. The ship's timbers were rotten and broken, but most of the hull and ribs remained intact, although they were encrusted with weeds, shells, and other undersea growths. As he carefully explored the wreckage of the ship, the diver came across two bronze cannons. If he had been topside, he surely would have let out a few yells and whistles, but underwater he just grinned and shook his head in disbelief.

"I've found the wreck of a Spanish galleon," he thought to himself, remembering pictures from his youth of the beautiful treasure ships of centuries ago. He also recalled learning that many fleet ships had gone down near the Florida coast, especially off the Keys—but there had also been talk of a wreck off Palm Beach.

"Maybe there's a treasure hidden down here," the diver thought as he tore through the weeds and barnacles and crawled into the center of the hull. There was so much sand that he began digging away as much as he could, and lo and behold, there, in front of his eyes, were rows and rows of blackened metal bars.

The diver could barely contain his excitement as he reached for his knife and scratched at the black surface. Then he saw the bright gleam of pure silver and knew he had stumbled onto a fortune—instant riches beyond his wildest dreams. He realized that

this was a job for a reliable salvage crew, and he immediately began thinking about a plan to recover the enormous amount of treasure.

"In the meantime," he thought to himself, "I'd better fix that cable." He located the break in the line and repaired it. When he surfaced, the diver checked and rechecked his bearings so he could easily relocate the wreck.

"It's been sitting there for hundreds of years, so I suppose it can wait a little longer," he thought. He carefully checked his figures: latitude, 26 degrees 45 minutes north; longitude, 79 degrees 55 minutes west.

Two years were to pass before the diver could raise enough money to finance his salvage expedition. He purchased a wrecking barge and salvage equipment, and hired a small but dependable crew. After researching the subject, the diver was convinced he had discovered the wreck of the Spanish galleon *Santa Margarita*. It sank in 1595 off the site of what is now Palm Beach, carrying a cargo of silver and gold valued at several million dollars.

(Note that this ship should not be confused with another Spanish treasure ship with the same name that went down in a hurricane off the Florida Keys in 1622.)

As preparations for the salvage operations began, Mother Nature stepped in, just as she had hundreds of years before when she sank the *Santa Margarita*. A savage hurricane roared up from the Caribbean and overwhelmed the salvage barge and its crew. Several men were killed, and all the equipment was lost in the storm. The diver was lucky to escape with his life.

After the hurricane passed, the diver descended to

the sea bottom to see how the wreck had fared
through the storm. He looked everywhere but could
not find a trace of the old ship. All around him the
diver saw nothing but smooth and unbroken sand on
the ocean floor. Apparently, the power of the storm
had shifted the sand on the sea bottom and completely buried the galleon.

The diver and the remaining men in the crew
searched the area for weeks before finally giving up.
He had come so close to recovering millions from the
Santa Margarita, and now he had nothing left but bit-
terness, disappointment, expenses, and an incredible
story to tell to his children and grandchildren.

Even today, the ancient Spanish ship may be
buried beneath tons of sand off Palm Beach, Florida.
Perhaps a recent and powerful storm has shifted the
sands on the ocean floor still another time, fully ex-
posing the wreck. Even now, the *Santa Margarita*
may wait undisturbed in the silent undersea world for
another diver to stumble across her millions in treasure.

Peg Leg's Gold

Peg Leg Smith was a genuine character of the Old West. Some say he was a prospector. Others say he was a trapper and a horse thief.

Born in Kentucky in 1801, Thomas L. Smith left home at an early age and traveled west looking for adventure. It's said that he lost his leg after being hit by hostile Indian arrows. After the wound became infected, he amputated his own limb with a skinning knife.

Smith inherited his bad temper from his father, and some people say that he often unstrapped his peg leg and used it as a weapon against opponents.

In the winter of 1828, Smith and his trapping companions completed a successful season and accumulated a large number of furs to sell. Their usual market was in Santa Fe, but this time Smith and a partner named Duke decided to take the furs west to sell in the pueblo of Los Angeles.

The hard part of the journey west was crossing the uncharted desert. Although Smith and his partner took as much water as they could, after three days of travel they were running short of the precious fluid. Smith began searching for water sources and noticed three small buttes, steep hills with flat tops, standing alone on the plain. One seemed to stand apart from the other two. Smith headed for the gulch between the buttes in the hope of finding water, but he was unsuccessful.

"Wait here for me, Duke," he told his partner. "Let me climb to the top so I can get a better view of the area. Maybe we'll be lucky and I'll spot some green growth where there's bound to be a freshwater spring."

Smith managed to get to the top of the butte but was so fatigued from the effort that he sat down to rest for a while. Looking around, he noticed that the hilltop was covered with small black stones. When he didn't spot any green areas in the distance that would indicate water, the angry and disgusted Smith grabbed a handful of the black stones and began throwing them around.

"Heavy little things," he thought to himself as he tossed them against the larger rocks. Smith picked one up and purposely broke it open. Inside was a small, reddish yellow stone.

"Gold?" he thought to himself.

He shrugged his shoulders. "Most likely copper," he decided, and put several of the stones into his pockets.

"If we don't find some water soon," he thought, "we'll die out here."

Peg Leg Smith didn't know it at the time, but his luck had already changed. The next night he and

Duke found a freshwater spring, and they soon reached Los Angeles, where the two sold their furs for a good price. Then Smith discovered at the local assay office (where metals are analyzed for gold and silver content) that the reddish yellow stones were actually gold nuggets, not copper. According to the assayer, the samples were a high-grade gold ore covered with manganese. Smith recalled that the top of the butte was blanketed with these strange stones—all in plain sight just waiting to be gathered up by a lucky prospector.

Thanks to Smith's fondness for alcohol and a good story, news of the discovery of a rich gold deposit in the desert east of Los Angeles spread like wildfire. Smith was said to have given directions to his lost gold in exchange for five dollars and a drink. But he had a tendency to make up so many false clues that after a while even he couldn't distinguish between fact and fiction.

Although he did search for the gold several times, he never could find those three buttes again. Soon liquor became the most important thing in his life, and Smith died of alcoholism (and frustration) in 1866 in San Francisco.

The search for Peg Leg Smith's lost gold didn't end with his death. Some prospectors have devoted their whole lives to finding the rich gold deposit, but so far all have met with failure. In *1001 Lost, Buried or Sunken Treasures*, F. L. Coffman places the gold in Riverside County, California, "between two and twenty-five miles northeast of Shavers Summit in a canyon on the slope of Eagle Mountain."

Smith himself once described it as "on the tallest of three hills, had a black top but was chalky yellow at the base . . . between Walker's and Warner's Pass,

147 miles from Victorville." Still another source says only that it's somewhere between Sante Fe, New Mexico, and Los Angeles.

The question is, when Smith crossed the Colorado River into California, at what point did he cross? Smith himself said he crossed at the Gila, which is the present site of Yuma, Arizona. But did he say it before or after alcohol had clouded his mind and memory? Treasure hunters starting from Yuma have been unable to locate the three buttes.

In his *Encyclopedia of Buried Treasure Hunting*, Karl von Mueller says that a Norwalk, California, man claimed to have found a can of bean-sized gold nuggets in 1956 in the Chuckawalla Mountains where three hills come together. Were these the three buttes Peg Leg Smith often talked about? Nobody knows for sure. In the meantime, the legend grows and the search continues.

The Tolling of
the Bell

The violent storm came up suddenly without warning in the late afternoon of October 9, 1799.

"Shorten the sails," screamed the captain to his crew, straining to be heard over the howling winds. "We'll try to ride it out!"

The nine-hundred-ton British warship *Lutine* was near Terschelling, one of the West Frisian Islands, off the coast of the Netherlands in the North Sea. On a special mission from England, the ship carried a cargo of gold and silver coins and bars worth about $10 million. A portion of the money was to be distributed to the British armies fighting the French in occupied Holland. The rest of the shipment would go to Germany, England's ally in the war against France. Few enemy vessels could hold their own against the superior speed, maneuverability, and firepower of the British warship, yet she was powerless in the face of Mother Nature.

Kelsun top of wind thing from dealing to follow
mentally on discovery and any several escape of the
movement in 19 try and hurt, roll and nation were

"The winds are increasing, Captain," reported the first mate. "I'm not sure how long we can hold the sails."

The storm worsened, and that night hurricane-force winds blew the sails completely off the beleaguered ship. The mighty warship was helpless in the storm.

"We're doomed, boys," the captain declared. "It's every man for himself."

Within minutes the *Lutine* drifted onto the rocks off Terschelling Island and began to take on water. Soon after, the warship broke apart and sank to the bottom of the sea. Three hundred crewmen lost their lives that night, and the enormous shipment of gold and silver went down with the ship.

The *Lutine* had been insured by Lloyd's of London, the famous insurance underwriting corporation, which ended up paying the British government more the $4 million for the total loss of the ship and its cargo. Although Lloyd's was desperate to salvage what it could of the *Lutine*'s treasure, the Dutch government staked a claim to the wreck since it was now located in Dutch waters.

Some of the lost treasure was recovered in the years immediately after the disaster. A few local villagers and fishermen carried away gold or silver bars or coins when the wreck was partially exposed during low tide, when the sea level was at its lowest point, but drifting sands prevented large-scale salvage operations. The Dutch returned the title to the wreck to England's King George IV in 1857, and the king promptly handed it over to Lloyd's of London.

By this time, the *Lutine* was buried beneath twenty or more feet of sand. Salvage attempts by Lloyd's resulted in the discovery of only a small portion of the treasure. In 1859 the ship's bell and rudder were raised to the surface. Both were taken to Lloyd's headquarters in London, where the rudder was made into a table and chair.

Since the mid-nineteenth century, several more salvage attempts have been made, but each has been hampered by either bad weather, shifting sands, or rough seas. An attempt in 1911 unearthed a five-foot layer of iron and cannonballs that had fallen into the treasure hold on top of the gold and silver.

Another try in 1933 netted several hundred thousand dollars' worth of gold and silver coins, which a Dutch salvage firm split with Lloyd's. An attempt by a German firm in 1933 failed to locate the treasure at all.

In 1938, a Dutch dredge brought up a single gold bar and coins worth over four thousand dollars, plus three cannon. The workmen determined that the *Lutine* had broken apart in the 139 years since it went down. That part of the ship which contained the treasure was no longer in the original location. The big question was, where and how far did the wreck drift?

No more serious attempts have been made to salvage the *Lutine*'s treasure since 1938. But Lloyd's of London has never forgotten the ship and her cargo. Since 1859, the *Lutine*'s bell has hung at the firm's main headquarters on Lime Street in London, and to this day whenever bad news occurs (such as a great shipping loss), the bell tolls once. When there is good news, the bell is rung twice.

You can be sure the *Lutine*'s bell will ring at Lloyd's of London on the day someone mounts another large-scale salvage attempt to recover the lost treasure. But the outcome of such a complicated operation remains uncertain. Will the bell toll once, or will it toll twice?

Of the $10 million in treasure lost at sea on that stormy night in 1799, only half a million dollars in gold and silver coins and bars has been salvaged. That leaves $9.5 million in treasure still waiting to be discovered on the sandy sea floor off the Netherland coast!

Peak of Frustration

Milton "Doc" Noss, a chiropodist (foot doctor) from Hot Springs, New Mexico, was deer hunting with his wife and friends one beautiful morning in 1937 when he became separated from his companions.

After a time, Noss returned to the group and casually took his wife aside. "You're not going to believe this," he whispered, "but I found a cave full of treasure on Victorio Peak."

It was shortly after he was separated from the group that Noss spotted an opening in the hillside. Something about it seemed out of place in the surrounding environment. He discovered that the narrow opening led to a cave, which in turn led to a vertical shaft. Noss climbed down and found himself in a large cavern filled with stacks of neatly piled black bars.

When Noss rubbed one of the bars, he saw a flash

of gold emerge from behind the black coating. His eyes widened. "Could it be?" he thought to himself. Had he discovered the legendary gold mine of Victorio Peak?

According to legend, Victorio Peak, located west of Alamogordo and east of Truth or Consequences, New Mexico, was supposedly the site of an old Indian mine containing a rich vein of gold. It was believed that a Spanish priest named LaRue mined millions in gold, which he made into bricks, in 1759 until he was finally discovered by Mexican authorities. Although LaRue and his cohorts were arrested and put to death, none of them revealed the location of the gold.

In the 1870s, more than a hundred years later, Apache Indians raided white settlers in the Victorio Peak area. It is believed that the Apaches stored the loot from these raids in the same hidden mine where LaRue had kept his gold bars.

As Noss's eyes became accustomed to the faint light of the cavern, he explored farther and discovered, in addition to the gold bars, piles of old coins and jewelry. Suddenly he jumped back in horror, his heart racing. He saw two skeletons chained to an iron ring in the ground. Not far from that grisly sight were the bones of still another person. When Noss saw the tufts of red hair on the skull, he began to feel a little sick and left the cave.

Later that day, he brought his wife, Ova, to the opening he had discovered in the hillside. "Wait for me here, and you'll soon get the surprise of your life," he told her.

Noss disappeared into the opening and a couple of hours later came back and presented Ova with handfuls of golden coins and jewelry. She couldn't believe

her eyes. "It was," she later told the *Albuquerque Tribune*, "the happiest moment in our lives."

For the next two years Noss returned frequently to the treasure cave, but he always went in alone, without Ova. It was illegal at that time to own or trade large amounts of gold, so Noss brought out eighty bars and reburied them in places only he had knowledge of. Although they were worth about twenty thousand dollars each, the gold bars would be useless to him unless the law changed and individuals were again allowed to own, sell, or trade gold (that finally happened in 1973).

Noss supported himself and his wife by selling some of the jewelry and other relics from the cave on the black market. According to Ova, Noss once showed her a gold crown consisting of 243 diamonds and a large ruby. Noss believed it to be the crown of the Mexican emperor Maximilian, who ruled in the 1860s.

According to the claim filed by Noss with the New Mexico State Land Office, the treasure lay in a series of caverns that intersected one another in the interior of the mountain. There were swords, guns, Wells Fargo chests, gold coins, thousands of gold ingots, and a number of human skeletons.

Ova had never seen the treasure cave and never knew where Doc Noss reburied the gold bars. When Noss divorced her in 1946, she filed separately for the legal right to the claims but was unsuccessful.

Noss continued to try to clear the other cave passages and took on partners to help him, but the partnerships always disbanded. Unfortunately, he finally took on one partner too many. In 1949, Doc Noss was shot to death by another of his partners, Charles

Ryan, who was acquitted of murder on the grounds that he fired in self-defense.

After her ex-husband's death, Ova Noss claimed all rights to the treasure, but she could never find the exact location. When the area became part of the federal government's White Sands Missile Testing Range in 1955, Ova was forced to leave, since the land was now off-limits to civilians.

In 1958 Captain Leonard Fiege and his friends were deer hunting on Victorio Peak. Quite by accident, he discovered a small cave leading to a shaft, which in turn led to a cavern filled with gold bars just like the ones found by Doc Noss twenty years before.

Fiege immediately filed a formal claim to the gold. But it wasn't until 1961 that he was allowed by military authorities to return to the area. The expedition was a failure regardless. It's unsure whether Fiege couldn't locate the cave entrance, whether the opening was completely blocked by dirt, or whether the gold was gone.

Fiege took a lie detector test that indicated he was telling the truth about discovering the treasure cave. In the meantime, Ova Noss believed the government was secretly trying to locate the mine and claim the treasure. She filed a suit in court claiming she was the rightful owner of the mine. In 1979, before the matter could be resolved, Ova Noss died. The government continued to deny civilians the right to search for the treasure. One group was given permission to explore Victorio Peak for one week in 1977, but even they came up empty-handed.

Does the treasure of Victorio Peak really exist? Did Doc Noss file a fictitious claim with the New Mexico Land Office? Was most of Ova Noss's later life involved in a wild-goose chase? Did she lie about her husband's treasure?

And what about Captain Fiege and the lie detector test? He and his friends swore they saw the gold. Did the military discover the treasure, confiscate it, and then try to cover up the incident?

There are many questions and very few answers.

Is it a tall tale or nothing but the truth? Is there really a fortune in gold on Victorio Peak? Until better evidence is produced, no one really knows for sure.

The Beale Codes

"Let's make camp here," declared the cowboy to his friends. "I think we could use a long rest and a hot meal after chasing buffalo all day."

"That is the biggest and fastest herd I've ever seen," said another of the men. "Did you notice that some of the bison have light-brown to dirty-white coats now that the weather's changed? They're worth more money."

"If we can ever catch up to the herd," the cowboy added.

Suddenly, one of the men who was collecting wood for the campfire started yelling, "I don't believe this! Everybody come here! See what I found!"

The man had noticed a shiny glint in the nearby rocks and went over to investigate. He took out his knife and scratched a rock's surface. "It's gold! I just found a vein of pure gold!"

The cowboy spoke quickly. "I want two of you to

ride back to Santa Fe and show Captain Beale. Bring him and the others back with you right away, because I think we're all going to be rich men."

It was March of 1817. Thomas Jefferson Beale and twenty-nine of his friends had left their homes in Virginia to hunt buffalo and grizzly bears on the western plains. The area around Santa Fe was Spanish territory, not yet a part of the United States. It was a place where gunplay was common and only the strong survived.

The men elected Beale their captain and headed west. They spent the winter in Santa Fe, and to avoid fights among the restless men, Beale sent out a group of nine to hunt buffalo.

Two of the men left immediately to bring Beale and the rest of the party back to their camp. It was located in a small ravine about 250 to 300 miles north of Santa Fe in the Sasquatch Mountains.

By the time Beale arrived, the other men had already started mining the gold ore and happily announced to their captain that they had also discovered a vein of silver in the area. Beale immediately took charge and organized the mining operation, hiring several local Indians to help. The group worked for a year and a half accumulating a large quantity of gold and silver.

"We've got to keep this a secret or this whole area will be swarming with prospectors," declared Beale to his men. It was decided that the treasure should be transported back to Virginia and carefully buried for safekeeping.

Beale and ten men in the group loaded the silver and gold into iron pots and made the long trip back east in 1819. They selected a spot in the Blue Ridge mountain range and, under cover of night, dug a hole six feet deep and deposited the pots, carefully covering them so no one could tell that the ground had been disturbed.

Beale returned to the mine in Santa Fe after spending some time in Lynchburg, Virginia, where he became friends with Robert Morriss, the owner of the hotel where he stayed. In 1821 Beale made another trip to Virginia to add more treasure to the secret burial vault and again visited his friend in Lynchburg. When Beale traveled west again in 1822, he left a locked iron box in Morriss's care.

Morriss received a letter several months later in which Beale explained that the locked box contained important papers, several of which could not be read without a special decoding key. Beale instructed Morriss to wait ten years if he did not hear from Beale and then open the box. He also noted that in ten years—specifically, in June of 1832—a friend of Beale's would send Morriss the key to the code so he could understand the papers in the box.

Thomas Jefferson Beale was never heard from again. He was presumed killed somewhere out west. One source stated that Beale's remains and those of his friends were eventually found in the Sasquatch Mountains; they were probably killed by thieves or by hostile Indians. No gold or silver was found in the area.

Years passed. The year 1832 came and went, and Morriss did not receive the key to Beale's code. He waited until 1845 to finally open the box. Inside were two letters and three series of numbers. The letters had been written by Beale in 1822 and explained how he and his friends had found the gold and silver mines and how they came to bury their riches.

In the letter, Beale asked Morriss to locate the trea-

sure and deliver portions of it to beneficiaries of the miners who were still living. In return for his trouble, Morriss was to keep a full share of the treasure.

The first series of numbers described the exact location of the gold and silver. The second series of numbers listed the specific contents of the vault, and the third series contained the names and residences of the beneficiaries. But Beale's friend had never sent Morriss the key to the code. Without the key, the numbers were meaningless!

For seventeen years, Morriss tried but failed to decode Beale's series of numbers. Finally, in 1862, an elderly and ill Morriss told his friend James Ward the whole story and asked him to continue to try to break the codes. Morriss made Ward promise to distribute half of the treasure to the miners' families and told him to keep the other half himself if he was successful.

Morriss died the following year, in 1863, but Ward kept working on the code. He believed each number represented a letter in a particular text, yet many different numbers represented the same letter. The big question was, which text? After years of work, Ward discovered one of the keys. It was the Declaration of Independence, written by Thomas Jefferson, the president for whom Beale had been named.

Ward numbered every word in the Declaration from 1 through 1,322. For example, the first phrase, consisting of seven words, is "When in the course of human events." The word *when* was number 1, so every time Ward found a number 1, he made it a *w*. The word *in* was number 2, so each time Ward found a number 2, he made it an *i*, and so forth; 3 was *t*, 4 was *c*, 5 was *o*, 6 was *h*, and 7 was *e*.

The second series of numbers was decoded at last!

The message read: "I have deposited in the County of Bedford about four miles from Bufords in an excavation or vault six feet below the surface of the ground the following articles belonging jointly to the parties whose names are given in number three herewith. The first deposit consisted of ten hundred and fourteen pounds of gold and thirty-eight hundred and twelve pounds of silver deposited November 1819. The second was made December 1821 and consisted of nineteen hundred and seven pounds of gold and twelve hundred and eighty-eight pounds of silver also jewels obtained in St Louis in exchange for silver to save transportation and valued at thirteen thousand dollars. The above is securely packed in iron pots with iron covers. The vault is roughly lined with stones and the vessels rest on solid stone and are covered with others. Paper number one describes the exact locality of the vault so that no difficulty will be had in finding it."

Unfortunately, this message told only what was buried, not where it could be found. Ward was never able to decipher the other two codes, and neither has anyone else. Over the years, thousands have tried, and all have failed. A group of code experts called the Beale Cypher Study Committee has also been unsuccessful.

If one of Beale's keys was the Declaration of Independence, what could the other two be? Keep in mind that Beale was a Virginian who lived in the early nineteenth century. What could he have read or memorized? Prayers, verses of the Bible, rhymes, a popular song of the day—who knows?

Will the Beale codes ever be deciphered and the treasure found? Perhaps with the help of advanced computers. In the meantime, your guess is as good as anyone else's.

Yo Ho Ho and
a Bottle of Rum

Cocos Island appears to be a place untouched by time—isolated, remote, and uninhabited. Its dense jungles and green vegetation combine to give one a sense of being suspended in the past.

A visitor would hardly be surprised to see a *Tyrannosaurus rex* poke its head above the treetops or to be able to watch King Kong scale the sheer rock face of the island's twin peaks. Perhaps one might come face-to-face with bloodthirsty pirates burying their stolen treasure.

It's common knowledge that King Kong is a purely fictional character, and whether or not dinosaurs once ruled Cocos Island is pure conjecture. But be assured of one thing: Murderous and brutal pirates have been burying their spoils on this small tract of land for hundreds of years! In fact, some believe Cocos Island was the model for Robert Louis Stevenson's classic, *Treasure Island.*

Located about 400 miles southwest of Costa Rica, in the Pacific Ocean, this island supposedly has more buried pirate treasure than any other location in the world. And more people have spent more money and more time trying to find that treasure.

In Chatham Bay, the main sea inlet on Cocos Island, the names and messages from long-dead generations of treasure seekers can still be seen carved in the big boulders that overlook the water. "SHIP INDIENCHIEF OF NEW LONDON CPT. BALEY MARCH 28 1848" and "SHIP ALEXDR. COFFIN D. BAKER NANTUCKET OCTO. 12 1833" are typical examples. One mysterious message has kept people guessing for more than a hundred years: "LOOK Y. AS YOU GOE FOR YE S. COCO." No one knows what it means or what clues it might contain for finding the treasures reputed to be buried on the island.

Most historians believe there are several treasures buried on Cocos Island, with a total estimated value of over $100 million. The hiding of the largest and most famous dates back to the 1820s. The revolutionary army of Simón Bolívar was threatening the Spanish colony of Lima, Peru, on the western coast of South America. The wealthy Spanish citizens and church officials in the Peruvian capital gathered their treasures together and chartered whatever ships were available to take their riches out of the country while they stayed behind.

A small merchant ship, the *Mary Dear*, captained by a man named William Thompson, was hired to carry the contents of the Lima cathedral to safety, away from the clutches of Bolívar and his revolutionists. The cargo included gem-studded golden crucifixes; silver and gold candelabras; solid gold chalices; rosaries of emeralds, pearls, and other gemstones;

large chests of gold and silver coins; and a life-size jewel-encrusted gold statue of the Virgin Mary.

Whether the captain gave in to the temptation of millions of dollars' worth of treasure, or the first mate and crew forced Thompson to go along with them, the *Mary Dear* made off with the treasure. It was hidden in a well-concealed cave on Cocos Island.

Thompson and the crew were soon arrested for piracy by the angry Spaniards, and all except the captain and the first mate were put to death. The officers were kept alive in order to guide the Spaniards to the treasure. But the two managed to escape into the dense jungles of Cocos before the secret of the treasure was ever revealed. Eventually, the captain and the first mate were rescued by a whaling ship that had stopped at the island for fresh water.

The first mate died soon after. But Thompson supposedly gave a map pinpointing the location of the treasure to his friend John Keating. Keating is said to have visited the island several times in the 1840s, coming away with small portions of the treasure each time. Keating died in 1882 and left his wife a chart of the treasure's location, although historians disagree as to its accuracy.

According to the chart, as published by author Harold T. Wilkins in his book *Treasure Hunting*, follow the bay to a creek that connects to a stream that flows inland. "Step out seventy paces, west by south, and against the skyline you will see the gap in the hills. From any other point, the gap is invisible. Turn north, and walk to a stream. You will now see a rock with a smooth face, rising sheer like a cliff." If you've followed the directions correctly, a small hole, large enough to insert a thumb and about five feet up from

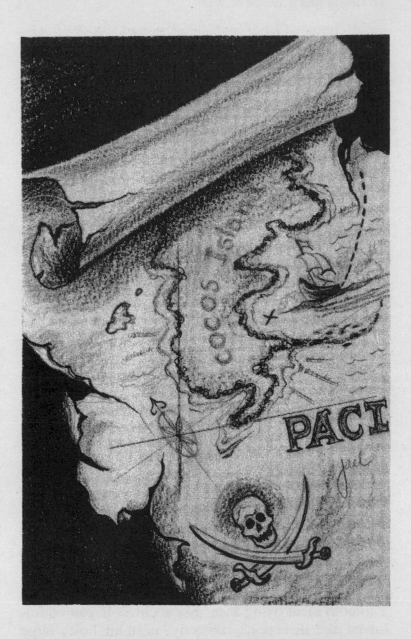

the ground, will be visible in the rock. Wilkins suggests twisting an iron bar in the hole which will reveal a door which opens on the treasure.

Easy as pie? A piece of cake? Tell that to the more than 450 treasure-hunting expeditions which have visited Cocos Island in search of the Lima treasure and have come away empty-handed—and with much smaller bank accounts!

The villain in the piece is Mother Nature. Torrential rains during the winter season have caused many landslides on the island over the years, resulting in major changes in the visual landscape there. It is now believed that the treasure cave is buried somewhere beneath thousands of tons of earth, rocks, and vegetation. Whatever streams, boulders, or other distinguishing geographical features may have existed in 1820 have completely changed or been obliterated since the *Mary Dear* first set anchor off Cocos Island 175 years ago. So, in effect, old maps, charts, and other clues are, for the most part, meaningless today.

In addition to the fabulous Lima Treasure, there are others reputed to be buried on Cocos Island. Pirate William Dampier was supposed to have hidden several treasure caches valued at over $60 million. The famous buccaneer, Edward Davis, may have also buried his booty on the island as did Sir Henry Morgan and Benito Bonito, two other well-known raiders of the high seas.

Although many historians are uncertain about the treasures of Dampier, Davis, Morgan, and Bonito, most agree that the Lima treasure does indeed exist somewhere on Cocos Island. However, according to author Wilkins, ". . . one might as well look for a needle in a haystack as hope to find it after this lapse of centuries."

Perhaps, one day, not so far in the future, someone will discover, quite by accident, that long sought after cave which holds one of the largest treasures on earth.

Swept Away

On or around the morning of October 12, 1216, King John of England surveyed the wide expanse of muddy water that blocked his path northward. It was called the Wash, and it was a shallow inlet of the North Sea with low, marshy shores located between Lincolnshire and Norfolk on the eastern English coast.

"If we go around, we'll lose two days or more," stated the king out loud. "Can we cross it?" he asked his advisers. "It looks shallow enough."

"The locals say this marshland can be treacherous, Your Majesty," answered one aide. "There are hidden spots of dangerous quicksand. And some even talk of sudden forceful waves that roll in from the sea."

"But they cross it frequently," added another adviser, "usually at low tide and with an experienced guide."

"There's no time for a guide. I'll cross first with

the troops," the king declared. "Then send the baggage train across."

John and his army had been on the march for weeks. The monarch was fighting to regain lost territory and to establish control over rebellious barons. Although King John was exhausted and ill from the military campaign, he was determined to stay on the move.

Seventeen years earlier, in 1199, John had assumed the English throne after the death of his brother, King Richard the Lion-Hearted. Richard's participation in the Crusades (Christian military expeditions to recover the Holy Land from the Muslims) had left the treasury bare. During his long absence, England was involved in a continuing war with France, and the country fell under the control of powerful barons. John's attempts to build up the royal treasury by excessive fines, taxes, and the seizure of his subjects' land resulted in civil war in England.

The year before, on June 19, 1215, at Runnymede, the strongest, most influential barons had forced the king to sign the Magna Carta, an agreement that guaranteed basic freedoms and rights to his subjects. Although the document itself was rather vague, some historians credit the Magna Carta with laying the foundation for future British democracy.

Civil unrest continued, but this major military campaign by John was slowly restoring order and money to his realm. As was the custom in the thirteenth century, the king traveled with his treasure and valuables in a baggage train of horse-drawn wagons.

No one knows for sure what happened that morning when King John's baggage train crossed the Wash. Perhaps the tide had not yet gone out, and without a guide the treasure-laden carts and wagons

were sucked into the quicksand. Maybe a sudden and violent wave of water, called a hygre or eagre, rolled through the Wash and swept away the men, horses, and carts of the baggage train.

Author Ian Wilson published Roger of Wendover's 1235 account of the incident in his book *Undiscovered*. According to Roger's *Flores Historiarum*, written several years before his death in 1235: "Heading for the north, [King John] lost, by an unexpected accident, all the wagons, carts, and packhorses, with the treasures, precious vessels, and all the other things which he cherished with special care; for the ground was opened in the midst of waves, and bottomless whirlpools engulfed everything, together with men and horses." Roger notes that the king barely escaped with his army and spent the next night at Swineshead Abbey.

Whether the king had already crossed the Wash or had taken a different route than his baggage train is not known for sure. But historians believe John witnessed the terrible loss of all his wealth and treasure, which was particularly bitter due to his efforts to rebuild England's treasury. He was already ill, and this final disaster broke his spirit. King John died a shattered man six days later, on October 18, 1216.

The treasure lost in the Wash more than 750 years ago consisted of gold and silver goblets, candelabras, jewels, crowns, pendants, robes, scepters, and other priceless royal regalia. Today, due to land reclamation and diversion of old waterways that once flowed into the Wash, the area where the treasure might be located is now dry land. Whatever relics still exist are believed to be buried under as much as twenty to thirty feet of sand.

Historians disagree as to the actual crossing point

of the baggage train. If a sudden and violent wave came out of nowhere, it could have swept the treasure farther upstream, making it even more difficult to pinpoint the location.

A search for King John's treasure in 1929 covered over 420 acres but yielded no clues to the mystery. A larger effort in 1932 also ended without success.

Finding the treasure of King John would be an enormous undertaking. If one were lucky enough to pinpoint the crossing location and also be able to finance the search, most of the valuables recovered would have to be shared with the British Crown. But the challenge and excitement of unearthing a long-lost and mysterious treasure would still be hard to resist.

Bronx Bonanza

Buried treasure in the Big Apple?

A fortune in gold and silver coins at the bottom of New York's East River?

A hidden bonanza of riches off East 138th Street in the Bronx?

Don't laugh. Many people believe a fortune lies waiting in the slime, ooze, and murky waters about fifty yards offshore.

The story begins during the American Revolutionary War. After defeating General George Washington and his colonial troops in the battles of Long Island, Harlem Heights, and White Plains in 1776, the British occupied New York City until English General Cornwallis surrendered his army at Yorktown, Virginia, in October 1781. Sometime in 1780, the H.M.S. *Hussar*, a twenty-six-gun British warship, set sail from England with a cargo of about $2 million in gold, silver, and copper currency. This money was to be used to pay the long-overdue salaries of the British soldiers fighting against the colonists in the American War of Independence.

Although historians differ as to the exact date, the *Hussar* most likely went down between 1780 and 1781 when she tried to navigate the dangerous riptides and rocky reefs of Hell Gate, at the junction of the Harlem and East rivers in New York. The ship sank to the bottom when treacherous currents forced her onto the rocks near Randalls Island and North Brother Island in fifty to seventy feet of water.

Historians also disagree as to whether the *Hussar* went down with the treasure on board. One relates that the money-laden ship was on her way to an unspecified location in Connecticut to pay the troops there. Another states that the *Hussar*'s destination was Newport, Rhode Island. Still another historian contends that the gold and silver coins had already been delivered to the commissary general in New York City before the *Hussar*'s last voyage. The big question remains unanswered. Did the warship go down with millions of dollars in her hold or nothing at all?

The first attempt to salvage the wreck of the *Hussar* was in 1818, when the ship's anchor and some of her guns were brought to the surface, but divers were unable to get inside the wreck and check for treasure. Several years later, a number of men used a diving bell to get near the ship's remains. During that attempt, a young man swam into the cabin and retrieved a bronze plaque and several other articles. As late as 1850, the location of the wreck was buoyed, so that other vessels could avoid the dangerous spot.

In the 1930s several unsuccessful attempts were made to locate and salvage the ship. The only attempt authorized by the federal government (which claims the *Hussar* and her contents) was made by inventor Simon Lake in 1935. Using a steel tube that descended into the river and a minisubmarine of his own invention with a glass window, Lake discovered three different wrecks in the vicinity of where the *Hussar* sank. But he, too, was unsuccessful—not only in confirming the *Hussar*'s identity but also in entering the holds of the remains of the ships.

The river bottom near Hell Gate is covered by assorted garbage and debris. Some older wrecks (other ships that have sunk in the East River) are buried under twenty feet or more of slime and mud.

Over the years, it is believed, the wreck of the *Hussar* has shifted in the fast-moving tides and currents of the East River. It's also quite possible that the treasure itself, which consisted mainly of gold and silver coins, has been scattered and buried all over the bottom of the river.

Until the rotting hull is located, identified, and explored, no one will know for sure if the *Hussar* went down with the British soldiers' payroll or an empty treasure hold. As time passes and the ooze, slime, and mud continue to accumulate, it will be harder and harder to verify whether there is a real Bronx bonanza or just a long-disputed myth.

The Cat's Meow

The two deep-red jewels were perfectly matched. Pure, clear, and second only to the diamond in hardness, these rubies were valued at half a million dollars.

According to F. L. Coffman in *1001 Lost, Buried or Sunken Treasures*, the two gems were first identified as the eyes of a sacred statue in a Korean temple dating back to A.D. 167. Then they mysteriously disappeared for several hundred years, only to surface again in the court of Suliman the Magnificent, sultan of the Ottoman Empire in the mid-sixteenth century. Apparently, Suliman gave them as a gift to one of his mistresses, and they were stolen by a thief who killed the unfortunate woman.

After another long disappearance, the rubies turned up in the possession of Louis XV, king of France from 1710 to 1774. Louis gave them as a present to his mistress, Madame de Pompadour. She, in turn, having more than her share of exquisite jewels and presumably in dire need of cash, sold them to a Russian nobleman whose name is not known.

More than a century passed, and in 1894, German police became aware that a well-known thief named Klaus Gudden had the two priceless gems in his possession. The Germans posted an all-points bulletin on Gudden and located him in a particular neighborhood of a major German city. Although he managed to outwit the authorities for several weeks, the police eventually closed in and captured him. Gudden was subsequently shot and killed while trying to escape.

The notorious thief did not have the rubies in his possession, and despite an extensive search, police could not find any clues leading to their location. Again, the two rubies had simply disappeared.

Coffman writes of a gem collector by the name of Michael Graves who decided in 1897 to trace the movements of Klaus Gudden in the days before his death in an attempt to find the jewels. By chance, Graves found out that on the exact day Gudden was captured and killed he had visited a small ceramics shop in the same neighborhood in which he was apprehended.

Upon questioning, the owner of the shop remembered the notorious thief because he had looked at the figures on display on the shelves but had instead selected a ceramic cat right out of the kiln, still soft and not yet hardened. When the owner tried to talk him out of his choice, Gudden insisted on the soft cat, and after paying for it had the proprietor set it aside for him, declaring he would pick it up later. Gudden was shot and killed several hours after, and the ceramic cat sat in the shop for two years, waiting for its owner to retrieve it.

Did Klaus Gudden hide the two priceless rubies

somewhere in the body of the still-soft ceramic cat? Michael Graves thinks he did.

The proprietor of the shop, figuring the customer would never return for the cat, included it in a special shipment to the United States in 1896. Graves traveled to America in an attempt to track down the figure. Much to his dismay and disappointment, he found that the shipment had been split up and sent to shops all over the country and that it was thus impossible to trace an individual ceramic piece. Graves gave up the search and returned to Germany, convinced that the cat contained half a million dollars' worth of rubies.

Today, one hundred years later, the infamous ceramic cat may be sitting on a shelf at a pawnshop or thrift store. It may even be at a garage sale, possibly chipped and cracked and marked "$5 or best offer."

There's a chance it was broken and the pieces were simply swept up and thrown into the garbage. Or perhaps it sits in someone's living room on the mantel or is used as a doorstop.

Look for a cat exactly eight inches tall from the base to the tip of the ears. It was originally yellow in color, in a sleeping position with its tail wrapped around its body and front paws. If you're lucky enough to spot a ceramic cat like this, carefully pick it up and examine it closely. Do you see a small dent or notch on its body where the two rubies might have been pushed into the soft clay? Turn it over and look at the base. Do you see any strange marks where the jewels may have been inserted?

Will the missing rubies ever turn up again? It's very possible since they have appeared and disappeared throughout history. In the meantime, keep your eyes peeled. You never know what treasure you may come across someday!

Pirate or Privateer?

In the eighteenth century the international political situation often determined who was a pirate or a privateer. Pirates robbed and often destroyed any unfortunate vessel they came across on the high seas. Privateers were hired by local citizens or members of a government. In time of war they fought the enemy by plundering commercial shipping.

Sometimes the political situation changed so quickly that a privateer could become a pirate without even realizing his sudden change of status. Take the case of Jack Quelch of New England. Quelch was first officer of the eighty-eight-ton privateer *Charles*, which was commissioned by Massachusetts governor Joseph Dudley in 1703. Her mission was to "war, fight, kill, suppress, and destroy any Pyrates, Privateers, or other Subjects and Vassals of Spain or France, and declared enemies of England."

The crew recruited to serve aboard the *Charles*

was a dishonest, greedy, and bloodthirsty group that mutinied before the ship had fully cleared the harbor. The crew dragged Captain Daniel Plowman, who had been ill, out of his cabin and threw him overboard. Then they chose First Officer Quelch as their new leader.

Quelch's first decision was where to sail. The new captain could have gone north to plunder ships from France, with whom England was then at war. Instead, contrary to his mission, he ordered the ship to steer for the east coast of South America and the richer ships of the Portuguese empire, which was not at war with England.

Eight months later the *Charles* had looted a total of seventeen Portuguese ships, and some historians believe she may have killed numerous Portuguese crewmen. Quelch and his crew collected more than two hundred pounds of gold dust, over two hundred bars of silver, and a large quantity of precious gems. On the way back to Massachusetts, the *Charles* came upon a stranded Spanish galleon and also took her cargo of gold and silver.

Some people believe that before sailing home to Marblehead Harbor, Quelch stopped off at the Isles of Shoals, ten miles off the coast of Portsmouth, New Hampshire. This cluster of seven small islands was said to be "infested by pirates" in the eighteenth century and is considered a place where many ships buried their stolen treasure. The famous pirate Blackbeard, among others, was said to have hidden treasure on several of these islands. Quelch and his crew supposedly buried two hundred bars of silver on the west side of Appledore Island, the largest of the Isles.

The *Charles* finally arrived home on May 20,

1704, and the crew went ashore to celebrate. When some crew members drunkenly boasted of the Portuguese ships they had plundered, word spread quickly of their exploits.

What Quelch and the crew hadn't known was that England had signed an alliance with Portugal while the *Charles* was away. So Quelch and his men had, in fact, been stealing from England's ally, and they were soon arrested for piracy!

Quelch claimed that Captain Plowman, before he died of his illness, ordered him to take command of the *Charles* and sail for Brazil, but other members of the crew testified to authorities that Plowman was thrown overboard in a mutiny. Quelch admitted to plundering the Spanish galleon but denied attacking the Portuguese vessels or taking part in the mutiny or in the murder of Plowman.

One of the sailors confessed that a large quantity of gold dust and gems had been given to Tom Larimore, captain of the *Larimor Galley*. Larimore and several *Charles* crew members were discovered on Star Island, in the Isles of Shoals, in the act of burying bags of gold dust.

In all, twenty-five *Charles* crewmen were arrested and went to trial. Eighteen others were never caught. Seven, including Jack Quelch, were hung for the murder of Plowman and for piracy on the high seas.

Some say Governor Dudley killed Jack Quelch because he wouldn't share the treasure with him. Dudley was able to keep sixty-five pounds of gold dust that the captured pirates had in their possession, but most of the loot remained unaccounted for.

What became of Quelch's treasure? It is still thought to be buried on the Isles of Shoals on either Appledore or Star Island, or on Snake Island off Cape

Ann, Massachusetts. In 1816 a man named Sam Haley, Jr., discovered four silver bars buried in the sand on Appledore; the silver bars were thought to be part of Quelch's treasure.

Citizens of Marblehead believe Quelch buried his treasure somewhere near their town landing. In fact, according to New England author Robert Cahill in his book *Pirates and Lost Treasures*, "Treasure Hunters Day was celebrated every May in Marblehead well into the 20th century!"

Heading for historical New England this summer? Who knows what surprises may be unearthed on one of those tranquil and picturesque islands off the New Hampshire and Massachusetts coastline. Happy hunting!

Guatavita Gold

The ceremony of the gilded man was reaching a feverish pitch. The frenzied procession of Chibcha Indians stretched all the way around the sacred lake of Guatavita, high in the Andes Mountains of Colombia, South America. Led by the noble class of priests, the Chibchas carried banners and burned incense and perfumes. Music filled the air, and bonfires blazed in the night.

The special yearly coronation ceremony that paid tribute to the goddess of the lake was about to begin. The crowd grew quiet as the king and his four honored attendants stepped forward. The Chibcha monarch was stripped naked before his people, and the attendants covered his body from head to toe with a sticky, gumlike substance. Next they sprinkled their ruler with gold dust so that even in the dark of night, with only the light from the bonfires, the Chibcha king glittered and sparkled. He had become the

gilded man, the anointed golden one, or what the Chibcha's Spanish conquerors called El Dorado, the man of gold.

The king moved forward slowly and stepped to the middle of a large raft that was anchored at the edge of the lake. As he stood quietly, his subjects took turns heaping gold, jewels, and other precious objects and ornaments at his feet until the raft was piled high with treasure.

The king's attendants joined him on the raft as it floated slowly to the center of the sacred lake. The Chibchas who lined the water's perimeter then turned their backs on their leader, who with help from his attendants threw all the gold and jewels into the water as an offering to the goddess. Then the king threw himself into the lake and wiped the gold dust from his body in a symbolic gesture of washing away evil and bad luck. The king returned to the raft, and as it floated slowly back to shore, thousands of Chibchas now faced the water and cast showers of gold and jewels into the depths of Lake Guatavita.

This ceremony or something similar was the basis for the legend of El Dorado that was retold and exaggerated by the Spaniards for hundreds of years. Many men, such as Sir Walter Raleigh of England, came to South America believing they would find an entire city of gold. Instead, they discovered Lake Guatavita, nine thousand feet above sea level, its bottom presumably covered with gold, jewels, and other precious objects. But how could this treasure be recovered? Many have tried over the years, but few have succeeded.

A Spaniard named Quesada, who conquered the Chibchas between 1536 and 1541, made the first attempt. He organized gangs of Indians to try to drain the lake by using buckets in the hope of salvaging the gold. After three long months of work, the water level, lowered by only nine feet, revealed some gold objects and precious stones. But Quesada gave up on what he thought was an impossible task.

In 1578 a Spanish merchant named Antonio de Sepulveda attempted to drain Lake Guatavita. He had eight thousand Indians cut a large channel in the lake's outer rim, draining off enough water to expose about fifty to sixty feet of the steep, muddy sides. Hundreds of gold figures were uncovered, as well as a large, egg-size emerald that eventually sold for $70,000 in Europe. But the channel blocked up again, and after the Spanish government received its share of the treasure, Sepulveda ran out of money.

In the early nineteenth century, Monsieur de la Kier of the Royal Institute in Paris predicted that billions of dollars' worth of treasure still lay hidden in Guatavita's lake bed. German explorer and scientist Baron Alexander von Humboldt concurred, declaring that the lake could hold millions of dollars' worth of emeralds and gold.

After a first failed attempt in 1898, a British company tried again in 1909. It succeeded in draining all the water from Guatavita by tunneling underneath the lake and drawing out the water from below. After years of work and many thousands of dollars, the project was finally successful. The lake bed was exposed, but instead of finding layers of gold and precious stones, the workers found twenty-five feet of mud and sludge. Although a few gold ornaments and jewels were discovered, the lake bed hardened in the heat and the company had no money left to continue the exploration. After so many years of work, they had found only $10,000 worth of treasure—not enough to keep the company from going bankrupt. Tropical rains soon refilled the lake to its original level.

It is said that an American diver discovered Chibcha death masks and gold jewelry in Lake Guatavita in 1932. In 1965 the Colombian government declared the lake a protected area, and further explorations have been banned without special permission from the government.

No one knows how much gold lies at the bottom of Lake Guatavita, but gold objects continue to be found in the area. Some people believe that whatever treasure the lake holds should remain there as a tribute to the Chibchas and their lost culture. They argue that the Indians intended the gold and jewels to appease the goddess of Lake Guatavita, and there the treasure should stay!

Others feel that retrieving the gold and ornamental art of the Chibchas would add to the limited knowledge there is of these Colombian Indians. The Chibchas were a highly developed tribe that practiced agriculture, mining, weaving, pottery making, and the casting of gold and copper objects.

Both sides in the argument make important points. But one thing is certain: Because of the Chibcha coronation ritual hundreds of years ago, the Spanish term *El Dorado*, which means "man of gold," has taken on a different meaning today. It refers to any place of fabulous wealth, a bonanza, or a gold mine. Perhaps someday you'll find your own El Dorado!

He Threw
Away a Fortune

Seaman. Explorer. First Englishman to sail around the world.

Hero. Adventurer. Romantic. Patriot. Pirate. Plunderer.

All these words describe Sir Francis Drake, the man who won fame and fortune in Elizabethan England by defeating the Spanish Armada (fleet of warships) and exploring the New World.

During his three-year voyage around the globe, Drake, captain of the flagship *Golden Hind*, navigated the Strait of Magellan (at the tip of South America) and explored the Pacific Ocean, the California coast, and the South Sea islands. Along the way, Drake looted one Spanish settlement after another and pillaged every Spanish treasure ship he intercepted. In this way, he helped break the power of Spain and establish British control of the seas.

It was December 1577 when Drake set sail from

England on his around-the-world voyage. Once through the Strait of Magellan, Drake sailed up the west coast of the South American continent. He ransacked Valparaiso and Coquimbo (Chilean seaports), and plundered a fleet of treasure ships at Callao, the major seaport of Lima, Peru.

Drake's fearsome reputation preceded him, for when the Spaniards recognized the *Golden Hind*, they abandoned their ships and fled to shore. Drake helped himself to tons of silver bars, gold ingots, gems, and pearls as the frightened Spaniards stood by and watched. He then set the ships adrift and started out after the jewel of the Spanish treasure fleet, the *Cacafuego*, which had sailed for Panama two days before.

Although it was heavily weighed down with treasure, the *Golden Hind* managed to catch up with the *Cacafuego*. The Spaniards surrendered without resistance after a cannon was fired across their ship's bow.

Drake discovered an incredible array of treasure on board the captured Spanish vessel, including eighty pounds of gold dust, tons of silver bars and bullion, and cases of gold, silver, and jeweled objects worth millions of dollars. It took several days to transfer the loot from the *Cacafuego* to the *Golden Hind*, which now sat dangerously low in the water from the weight of the precious metals. A sudden violent storm could have proved deadly to Drake's ship, so he sailed to Cano Island (now called the Island of Plate), in the Pacific off the coast of Ecuador, for repairs.

At the island, Drake divided the treasure among his crew, supposedly using a washbowl to hand out gold and silver coins. Each man received sixteen bowlfuls!

They were all so wealthy and the treasure was so heavy that they decided that a portion had to be left behind if the *Golden Hind* had any chance of returning to England safely. Instead of burying the extra treasure on Cano Island, they threw forty-five tons of it overboard into the sea. It is said they could see the shiny gold and silver coins gleam in the clear water as they sank to the bottom.

Drake continued his circumnavigation of the globe and finally arrived back in London in September of 1580, presenting Queen Elizabeth with a good-sized portion of the treasure. He was welcomed as a hero and knighted by the queen herself.

Although word eventually spread of the cast-off treasure at faraway Cano Island, few attempts have even been made to recover it, despite the fact that the coins are supposedly located in shallow water with a hard, sandy bottom. It is said that the famous seventeenth-century pirate Edward Davis once salvaged about fifteen hundred silver coins one afternoon about a hundred years after Drake's crew threw them overboard.

The only other known attempt to recover the rest of the Drake treasure occurred in 1933, during the Great Depression in America. An English seaman who lived in South America constructed an inexpensive type of dredge for his small towboat and sailed for the Island of Plate. As the dredge brought up load after load of sand from the sea bottom, the excited crew found hundreds of gold and silver coins and other objects of precious metal. The Englishman and his crew managed to salvage eighteen tons of the treasure before the dredge broke down and the operations ended.

Although Drake's discarded treasure is small in

comparison with others, it is still thought to be worth more than half a million dollars. Perhaps the payoff isn't big enough for serious treasure hunters, who often spend much more than that for specialized equipment, supplies, a ship, and crew.

If reports are accurate, nearly twenty-seven tons of treasure still lie on the bottom of the sea near the Island of Plate. Imagine how exciting it would be to discover four-hundred-year-old coins and other precious objects once owned by Sir Francis Drake himself!

Dr. Thorne's
Apache Gold

In the year 1852, a doctor named Thorne and six other men were traveling east from California when they were attacked by Apaches at the Arizona stage depot of Maricopa Wells. Five of the men were killed in the battle and one escaped. Dr. Thorne was captured and taken prisoner when he made it known to them that he was only a "medicine man" and meant no harm to anyone.

The Apache camp, located near the Salt River at the base of the Mazatzal mountain range (about eighty miles northeast of Phoenix), was surrounded by rocky wasteland and afforded no possibility of escape for a man on foot.

According to Leland Lovelace in his book *Lost Mines and Hidden Treasure*, the Apaches allowed Dr. Thorne to freely move around their camp since escape was impossible. He began to treat people who were sick or in distress using medicine and supplies from his black bag.

As the months passed into years, Dr. Thorne became an accepted member of the Apache community. But he eventually got homesick for his own people and asked the chief for permission to return to the white settlements. A powwow was held by the Apache leaders, who had mixed feelings about Dr. Thorne. They were grateful for the help he had given their people. He had earned his freedom, but they secretly hoped he would stay on with them. Chief Red Sleeves decided to let the medicine man go free but did not give him a horse or weapon, hoping to discourage him from setting out on foot in the wilderness alone and unarmed.

Dr. Thorne accepted his freedom but decided to stay on, at least temporarily, with the Apaches. To show their faith in and acceptance of the white medicine man, they agreed to share with him the secret source of Apache gold. The Indians sometimes used the yellow metal for ornamental purposes and occasionally made gold-tipped arrows. They had no real use for the gold, but they were aware that white men treasured this metal above all other things.

One day the Apaches blindfolded Dr. Thorne, placed him on a pony, and led him on a long and rocky journey. When he at last was able to remove his blindfold, the doctor was amazed at what he saw.

Lovelace described Dr. Thorne's astonishment in his own words. "I was standing in a narrow canyon," the doctor related. "At my feet there was a vein . . . at least eighteen inches wide, cutting across the canyon and running up the other side. The sun was shining on the vein and it was . . . pure, shining, naked gold."

Thorne realized he would someday want to come back to the canyon alone and tried to look for landmarks without attracting the attention of the Apaches. Glancing up at the skyline, he saw Four Peaks Mountain but wasn't sure which side he was facing. Then he was blindfolded again and brought back to the Apache camp.

A short while after seeing the canyon of gold, Dr. Thorne finally left the Apaches. He returned to the white settlements after a long and difficult trek across the wilderness. Thorne planned to return to search for the gold, but it was years before the Apaches ceased hostilities and he could return to the area safely.

When the aging doctor finally returned, he could not locate the vein of gold. He made trip after trip, from every direction and angle, and still was unsuccessful. But Thorne didn't give up until age and illness forced him to stop what had become the main focus of his existence. "The search for the gold had become his life," wrote Lovelace, "and when that search ended, he died."

Over the years, many people have tried to discover what became known as the Lost Doctor Thorne Mine, but without success. Most prospectors disagree as to its location. Some believe it lies in the White Mountains near the Black River. Others say it's somewhere between the Four Peaks, Weaver's Needle, and Red Mountain in the Superstition range. Still others search near the Salt and Verde rivers.

"The narrow canyon," concluded Lovelace, "with its great mass of virgin gold awaits him [or her] who finds it."

No Mercy

"Nobody but me and the Devil knows where my money is buried," declared Edward Teach, otherwise known as Blackbeard the pirate. "And the one what lives longest will get it all!"

Some say he was the cruelest, most ferocious pirate to sail the Atlantic coast in the eighteenth century. His savage and frightening appearance helped to add to his evil reputation. Some of his victims surrendered on their knees at the very mention of his name, but if they were hoping for mercy, they never received it.

This was a man who let his hair and beard grow very long, braided them in sections, and tied the braids with red ribbons. He wore broad belts—called bandoliers—one over each shoulder, crisscrossing over his chest. The belts had pockets for ammunition and six ready-to-use matchlock pistols that he lighted with long matches he carried under his hat.

Blackbeard ruled his men by keeping them afraid and in awe of him. Once he dared his crew to hang with him by the neck at the end of a rope to see who could last the longest. Another time he called the crew into his cabin one night, lit a sulfur pot, and challenged them to breathe in the choking fumes for as long as they could stand it. It was Blackbeard who remained in the cabin the longest. While the others fled, coughing, blinded, and gasping for air, he stood alone laughing. As a joke, he once fired his pistol under a table and accidentally crippled his first mate by destroying his kneecap.

Blackbeard had fourteen wives and forty children, give or take a few. It's said that he did away with several of his spouses. In fact, one of his treasure chests dug up along the Virginia coast was said to contain not gold doubloons but the skeleton of Mrs. Blackbeard number 7!

It was Blackbeard who originated the custom of shooting the men who helped him bury his booty and throwing one of their bodies on top of the treasure chest. That way only Blackbeard knew the exact location of his riches—and in case anyone dug deep enough to uncover the skeleton, he would probably be superstitious enough not to dig farther.

The fearsome pirate frequented the coves, rivers, and inlets of the Atlantic coast from about 1713 until 1718. Here he would hide from pursuers, repair his ships, and bury his treasure. Blackbeard is believed to have hidden his loot in various places, including the Isles of Shoals, off the New Hampshire coast; Amelia Island, off Florida (where gold doubloons have been found); and New Providence Island, in the Bahamas, which he used as a base.

A large quantity of Blackbeard's gold may be hid-

den on an island ten miles off the Georgia coast and
fifty miles south of Savannah. It is appropriately
named Blackbeard Island, and though many have
tried to locate his treasure, none have been successful.

Author Ben Ames Williams once wrote that "no
one can set foot on the shore without being conscious
of the ancient mystery of the place; without feeling
. . . a whispering fear."

By 1718, Blackbeard had four armed ships and
nearly four hundred men at his command, plundering
shipping from the Virginia coast south through the
Central American coast. He once blockaded the harbor at Charleston, South Carolina, and held colonial
officials for ransom.

North Carolina governor Charles Eden allowed
Blackbeard safe haven and pardoned him in return
for a share of his plunder. But Virginia governor
Spotswood offered a hundred-pound reward for the
"apprehending and killing of Edward Teach, com-
monly called Blackbeard."

In November 1718, two British warships under the
command of Lieutenant Robert Maynard managed to
surprise Blackbeard and two of his ships at low tide
in Ocracoke Inlet, North Carolina. True to his image,
Blackbeard refused to surrender, and he and his
twenty-two crewmen jumped aboard the British ships
and fought furiously in hand-to-hand combat with
cutlass and pistols though totally outnumbered.

Bleeding from dozens of stab wounds and five
musketballs, Blackbeard refused to go down until
Lieutenant Maynard finally slit his throat. Those pirates who were still alive immediately gave up when
they realized their ferocious captain was finally dead.

Needing proof to claim the reward and to show

officials that the larger-than-life pirate was really dead, Maynard sliced off Blackbeard's head and hung it on a pole on the front of his ship!

It's been more than 275 years since Edward Teach died, but his legend and the dream of finding his lost treasure live on today. Fortune hunters still seek Blackbeard's booty all along the Atlantic seaboard. They search for small, nearly hidden inlets or oceanside caves off the coast of Florida, Virginia, Georgia, the Carolinas, and places farther north. They hunt for locations where a notorious pirate like Blackbeard could find a safe haven and perhaps bury a treasure chest or two before setting sail again.

The gold awaits ye, matey.

All That Glitters

Greed. Hate. Murder. Gold.

All four figure prominently in the history of the mysterious Lost Dutchman Mine. The story of what some call America's most notorious hidden treasure has more intrigue, violence, drama, and bloodshed than any screenplay Hollywood writers could create.

Panoramic long exterior shot of the Superstition Mountains in a wilderness area east of Phoenix, Arizona. Cut to slow camera close-up of rattlesnakes and a white human skull amid jagged rocks and dry washes.

To the Apache Indians of the Southwest, these mountains are a sacred and mystical place, home to their powerful thunder god. In 1845, the wealthy Peralta family of Mexico came to this dangerous wilderness and discovered great quantities of gold.

Exterior close-up of Sombrero Peak, known today as Weaver's Needle. Move camera slowly back to include shot of busy mining operation. Close-up of miners pushing wheelbarrows full of rocks rich with gold out of the mine opening. Pan to others breaking the rocks down, washing and sifting out the gold dust using cradles, and packing it up for shipment.

The Peraltas mined millions of dollars' worth of gold from the rich veins of ore they had discovered. But it all ended one day in 1848 when Apache Indians, angry that their sacred land had been violated, attacked and killed the miners in an ambush. Several of the Peraltas managed to quickly cover the entrance to the mine before the Indians could get to them.

Exterior long shot of angry, hatchet-carrying Indians attacking and killing the surprised miners. Pan to burros carrying gold-filled saddlebags, the animals becoming frightened by the sudden onslaught and galloping off into the hills.

For years after the massacre, saddlebags of gold dust were found by local settlers throughout the area, the last discovered in 1914.

Wide-angle camera shot of grizzled miner with several burrows laden with prospecting tools and supplies.

The mine lay undisturbed until about 1870, when a German mining engineer named Jacob Walz arrived on the scene. Word spread quickly that Walz, known as the Dutchman, had discovered the lost Peralta mine. Though many tried to follow Walz to his bonanza, no one succeeded. It is said that Walz murdered anyone who got too close to his gold.

Medium exterior shot of Walz circling back, surprising, and shooting two men who had trailed him to the vicinity of the mine. Dissolve to exterior shot of Walz, under cover of night, secretly visiting the mine and packing his saddlebags with gold dust.

By 1879, Walz had taken on a partner, a fellow German named Jacob Weiser, who shared the riches of the mine with him. But Weiser was eventually attacked and killed by Apache Indians. Walz killed his own nephew Julius, and is suspected of killing several others in order to protect his secret.

Exterior medium shot of Walz arguing with younger man near the mine entrance. As the younger man turns to walk away, Walz draws and shoots him in the back. Then, without emotion, he slings the body over one of the burros, grabs a shovel off the ground, and walks with the burro slowly into the hills.

Jacob Walz died in 1891, but not before he confessed to murder and described the location of the hidden mine to one of his neighbors, who had helped nurse the dying miner.

Interior medium shot of the aged Walz in his deathbed. A woman is leaning over the old man, trying to hear his very faint last words. Camera moves to extreme close-up of Walz's face as he speaks. "There are two veins of nearly pure gold," says the dying man. "Look near Weaver's Needle, where the tip of the needle's shadow rests at four o'clock, facing west."

Although Weaver's Needle was the name of a particular jagged peak, Walz's other directions were too vague to allow people to locate the mine entrance. But that didn't stop thousands of would-be prospectors from searching for the gold anyway—all without success.

At the turn of the century, a man named Charles Hall discovered gold in the Superstition Mountains, but not in the area thought to be the location of what was now referred to as the Lost Dutchman Mine. Hall's mine was successful for a short period of time before a mud slide covered the site in a rainstorm. Although several attempts were made, the gold vein could not be retraced and the mine was abandoned.

Exterior long shot of working mine site. Dissolve to night long shot of heavy rainstorm with thunder and lightning, then medium shot of landslide moving down the mountain and covering the mine entrance.

A man named Adolph Ruth came to the Superstitions in 1931 with what he believed was a map pinpointing the location of the Lost Dutchman Mine. After speaking to local ranchers, he was never seen alive again. At the end of a long search, his remains were finally discovered. Ruth had been shot and decapitated. There was no sign of any map, but in a notebook next to Ruth's head were written the Latin words *vene, vidi, vici,* which translated means "I came, I saw, I conquered."

Exterior medium shot of a man dressed for camping, asking directions at a local ranch. Dissolve to the remains of a deserted wilderness camp. Camera slowly moves to a close-up of a headless body dressed in camping clothes, and then pans to a spot several hundred yards away. Camera zooms in to extreme close-up of a head with two obvious bullet holes in the forehead. Next to the head is an open notebook with writing in it.

Had Adolph Ruth discovered the Lost Dutchman Mine? Was that why he was murdered and the map stolen?

Exterior medium shot of the entrance to a partially hidden cave. Move camera slowly through the small opening that remains and into the dark interior of the mine itself. Move camera to close-up, and then extreme close-up, of a hint of shiny gold in the rocky wall. Then slowly move the camera back to reveal a large, thick vein of twinkling ore, which catches the small amount of light and sparkles a golden color on the screen.

Treasure hunters are still attracted to the Superstition Mountains in Arizona, where they hope to find the elusive treasure of the Lost Dutchman Mine. But does it really exist? Many people think so.

With the mine's history of greed and bloodshed, however, it's best to be fully armed and ready for trouble if you decide to give prospecting for it a try—and don't forget to watch your back!

Do You Know the Way to the *San Jose?*

"Admiral, we've sighted the Spanish fleet," the first officer reported, hardly able to contain his excitement. "Seventeen ships in all!"

"At long last," replied Admiral Charles Wager, commander of the seventy-gun H.M.S. *Expedition* and in charge of the British forces at Jamaica. "We're only interested in the three main ships, the ones carrying treasure. Signal the *Portland* and the *Kingston* to intercept the *almiranta* [vice-admiral and second in command of the fleet]. We'll close in on the *capitana* [the admiral or flagship of the fleet]. Order the men to assume battle stations immediately."

It was May 28, 1708, and Admiral Wager was in search of Spanish plunder off the coast of Columbia, South America. Convoys of treasure ships from the sixteenth through the early nineteenth centuries were the richest vessels to ever sail the seas. They were used to transport tremendous cargoes of gold, silver, and gems from the colonies of the New World back to Spain.

The vessels were large, unwieldy warships called galleons that weighed from 1,500 to 2,000 tons. They were three-masted with square sails. Most galleons had two decks, 150 to 185 feet long, with thirty to forty-five guns on either side above the waterline (broadsides). Spanish galleons were often top-heavy and overloaded with cargo. They were limited in maneuverability and frequently fell prey to the lighter and faster English vessels.

It was a long and dangerous voyage back to Spain for the treasure convoys. Between 1500 and 1820, hundreds of Spanish treasure ships were wrecked and millions of dollars' worth of precious metals were lost to the bottom of the sea. Convoys had to deal with fierce currents, shallow coral reefs, and unpredictable weather—not to mention pirates and the naval vessels of rival countries.

The speedier *Expedition* steadily closed in on the *capitana*, whose name was *San Jose*. Wager's faster vessel was nearly alongside the Spanish galleon when both ships began firing at each other at close range. Furious fighting continued for over an hour, until a British shot struck the Spanish vessel's powder magazine (where ammunition and explosives are stored). There was a huge explosion and the stricken ship, enveloped in flame, sank in seconds, taking its huge treasure down with her.

The *Expedition* suffered minimal damage, and Wager began to pursue the Spanish fleet's third galleon, the *gobierno* (which usually carried the highest ranking military man in the convoy), whose name was not known. In a battle that lasted over four hours, the smaller English ship emerged victorious as the *gobierno* finally surrendered.

While Admiral Wager was busy adding up the value of the chest of gold coins and silver bars on the captured Spanish *gobierno*, the *almiranta*, the *San Martin*, managed to escape the *Portland* and the *Kingston*. Both British warships gave up the chase to avoid entering the shallow waters of the Salmedina Shoals. The two captains of the British ships were later relieved of their commands for allowing the Spanish galleon to get away.

The value of the cargo of the sunken *San Jose* has been estimated at three to seven million pesos (about $482,000 to $1,124,000). With the sinking of the *capitana* and the capture of the *gobierno*, the blow to the Spanish economy was enormous. Admiral Wager was promoted to rear admiral by the British government, and when he returned to England in 1709 he was knighted by the queen.

There have been no salvage attempts on the *San Jose* because of disputes as to the exact location of the wrecked galleon. Some say she sank near the shallows of Salmedina. Others claim she went down in the vicinity of the Bancos del Tesoro (Treasure Banks), a coral ledge near the Columbian shelf off tiny Baru Island. Depths here range between 100 and 200 feet.

Before a search can begin, any diver or treasure seeker must have a permit for exploration and a separate license for salvage from the Columbian authorities, who permit very few treasure hunts.

Only eleven of the *San Jose*'s original crew of 600 survived the explosion that sent her to the bottom of the sea. The bones of 589 crewmen, together with a huge cargo of gold and silver, are entombed together on the ocean floor in this wreck, which some say is one of the largest undiscovered treasures in the Western Hemisphere.

The Lost San Saba/ Bowie Mine

"Where did those Indians get bars of silver to trade?" asked Jim Bowie, a recent arrival to San Antonio, in West Texas.

It was 1829, and Americans were pouring into this Mexican-controlled territory and organizing settlements there. Bowie, the famous scout and fighter known for his expert use of the knife that even today bears his name, was always ready to take a chance at finding a fortune.

"Many have tried to learn the secret of their wealth, *señor*," explained one resident of San Antonio. "Once or twice a year, Xolic, their chief, leads his people here to barter. They are Lipan Indians, a branch of the Apaches, and each time they come, they always bring silver with them."

"There must be a rich vein in the Llano region where the Lipan Indians live," remarked Bowie to the man. "Maybe it's the lost San Saba Mine, the hill of silver," he said with a laugh. To himself he thought, "And I aim to find it."

Bowie planned to befriend the Lipan Indian chief and immediately sent back east for a beautiful silver-plated rifle to offer him. Impressed with Bowie's generosity, Xolic held a powwow at San Pedro Springs, and Bowie was adopted into the tribe. He spent months living with the Lipans, gaining their trust. Bowie chased buffalo, speared wild cattle, and fought tribal enemies with the best of them. His reputation as a fearless warrior soon grew among the Indians.

Finally, the Lipans showed him the secret of the silver bars. It's uncertain whether Bowie was shown a natural vein of silver ore or a huge stack of silver bullion, mined and hidden by Spaniards who had once occupied the area. Whatever Bowie saw impressed him so much that almost immediately afterward he left the Lipans and rushed back to San Antonio.

Bowie quickly organized an expedition to return to the Llano region, where he planned to forcibly take over the silver. In the meantime, Chief Xolic died, and his successor, Tres Manos, accused Bowie of betrayal and treachery.

On November 2, 1831, Bowie led a party of eleven men—including his brother, Rezin Bowie, and a friend, Cephas Ham—back to find the mine. Before the men reached their destination, they were attacked by a large Indian war party while camped near a thicket adjacent to a creek. The 164 Indians outnumbered Bowie and his men, but the Americans had the advantages of a good defensive location and superior firepower.

The fight lasted all day, and when the dust cleared,

50 Indians were dead and 35 were wounded. Only one of the Americans was killed, and three were wounded. Bowie returned to San Antonio and immediately began to organize a second expedition. Supposedly, he returned to the area but was unable to locate the treasure.

The Texan war for independence broke out in 1835, and on March 6, 1836, the name of Jim Bowie became etched in American history when he and about 180 others died defending the Alamo (a mission that had been converted into a fort). Many people believe he died without revealing what he knew about the location of the Lipan treasure. Thereafter, it was often referred to as the Bowie Mine, and many feel the Lost San Saba and Bowie mines are one and the same.

When Bowie first noticed the Lipan Indians and their bars of silver, the lost San Saba Mine was already a legend in West Texas. It all began in 1756, when Don Bernardo de Miranda, lieutenant general of the Spanish province of Texas, explored the Llano region near Honey Creek and discovered a hill of silver.

Miranda wrote, "The mines ... are so numerous that I guarantee to give every settler in the province ... a full claim." Local Apaches told Miranda there were even "more and better mines" in the area. Miranda recommended that the Spaniards build a fortress (or *presidio*) to oversee and protect the mining operations from hostile Indians. Before a decision was made, however, Miranda set out on a second expedition to bring back a larger ore sampling and was never heard from again.

No one knows what became of Miranda, but the story of the hill of silver lived on. It began to be called the San Saba Mine because of its location near the river of the same name. Over the next fifty years, official reports continued to be filed on the richness of ore in this area, but discontent with Spanish rule—and the Mexican revolution of 1810, with its subsequent political upheaval—prevented any government action from being taken.

After Jim Bowie's involvement in searching for the mine, many others claimed to have found the lost treasure, including a man named Harp Perry. Perry said he mined and then buried a large amount of gold as well as silver. But after returning years later to claim it, he was unable to find the spot because the landmarks in the area had changed.

A rancher named Grumble was said to have met a Mexican woman who had befriended the Indians and knew the exact location of the mine. But Grumble was shot dead in a gunfight before he could be taken to the site.

A Spaniard named Aurelio Gondora supposedly possessed a treasure map that his father had given him that pinpointed the mine as being close to the junction of a creek and the San Saba River. Gondora showed the map to a friend named Merchant, but the map was stolen and Gondora was stabbed to death before he and Merchant could take any action. Merchant tried to find the mine on his own but failed.

Over the years, many others have tried to locate the treasure, but they too were unsuccessful for one reason or another. Does this lost mine really exist, or has the story been changed and exaggerated over the years to the point of fantasy?

Whatever the case, the endless possibilities of riches and wealth continue to lure men and women into the search for that elusive hill of silver in West Texas.

Pirate of the Gulf

Jean Laffite always avoided the word *pirate*. Instead, he described himself as a "gentleman smuggler and a privateer." A story is told about a man named Grambo who once declared that Laffite and his men were all pirates. Upon hearing this, Laffite calmly pulled out a pistol and shot Grambo through the heart. Though many might have thought it, no one called Laffite a pirate to his face again!

Born in Europe in 1780, Laffite and his brother Pierre were owners of a successful blacksmith shop in New Orleans at about the time of the Louisiana Purchase in 1803. By 1810, Jean had become the leader of a band of smugglers off the Barataria coast, south of the city. These Baratarians were issued authorization letters from several Latin American countries to plunder Spanish shipping, and for a time France and the United States authorized privateers like Laffite to attack English shipping.

The goods, treasure, and even shipments of slaves obtained from Spanish and English vessels were sold secretly duty free and at lower prices to buyers from New Orleans as well as to clients from Memphis and St. Louis. Laffite and his gang of smugglers were so successful that in 1813 American merchants and businessmen of New Orleans joined together to protest to the government that Laffite was taking away their business.

Governor Claiborne of Louisiana claimed the Laffite brothers were "bandits and pirates" and offered a reward of $500 for Jean's arrest and delivery. Laffite retaliated by offering a reward of $15,000 for the arrest and delivery of Governor Claiborne to him!

The United States had declared war on England in the War of 1812. In September 1814 the British secretly offered Laffite $30,000 in cash and a captain's rank in the British navy if he would help them capture New Orleans. Laffite stalled for time and informed U.S. officials of the British offer. He also volunteered his services in the defense of the city. Although at first reluctant, General Andrew Jackson accepted Laffite's offer and placed the Baratarians in charge of two important defensive positions.

After the battle was won and the British were defeated, Jackson praised the courage and loyalty of Laffite and his men. Soon after, President James Madison issued a full pardon to all Baratarians who had fought in the Battle of New Orleans.

Laffite moved to Galveston Island, Texas, and resumed the business of selling plundered goods and slaves at low prices. For several years, Laffite reigned as "Lord of Galveston Island," living in luxury from the spoils of Spanish treasure he had obtained. It was once said that gold doubloons were as plentiful there as biscuits. Laffite usually received a fifth of whatever booty his men brought in, and it is believed that portions of treasures were buried all over the island for future use.

Laffite plundered mainly Spanish shipping, but occasionally his men erred and attacked American vessels. After several offenses of this kind, a Lieutenant Kearney, representing the U.S. government and commander of a naval warship, appeared at Galveston Island one day in 1820 and politely but firmly ordered Laffite and his men to leave.

Laffite left, taking much of his accumulated booty and burying the rest in various hidden locations along the coast. He never returned to the United States and is reported to have died in Mexico in 1826.

But Laffite's memory lives on, and his treasures have been sought in every inlet and island throughout the Gulf Coast. One Laffite treasure hoard is supposedly located in the waters off Padre Island, Texas. Apparently, a Spanish treasure ship was forced onto the rocks there by Laffite's men, and to this day its remains are believed to be at the bottom of the sea, still undiscovered, under large amounts of sand and silt.

Another Laffite treasure cache is thought to be buried near the mouth of the Lavaca River in Texas. A heavy chest containing a million dollars in gold was buried about a quarter of a mile east of the river in a grass flat. Laffite marked its location by burying a brass rod with the top foot sticking out above ground. Many people have searched for the treasure but could never find it.

Supposedly a sheepherder in the Lavaca River area was watching over a group of horses when he came across the brass rod and pulled it up out of the ground. Later that night the man mentioned the rod to his employer. The rancher had knowledge of the Laffite treasure, and the next morning he asked the sheepherder to lead him back to the exact spot where he'd discovered the rod. Unfortunately, the man was never able to find the spot again. The land was covered everywhere by coarse, thick grass, and since he hadn't marked the hole, he became confused as to its exact location.

In 1870 a farmer named Bundick in Lavaca County went turkey hunting and accidentally stumbled over a pile of bricks half covered by dirt and debris. He took one brick home to show to his brother. It was discovered to be pure silver and was thought to have been placed there by Laffite's men. The Bundicks tried to locate the bricks again, but they were unable to find them. Over the next fifty years, several people apparently stumbled upon these bricks, but each time they were unable to return to the cache.

Still another Laffite treasure is reportedly buried in a spot overlooking the mouth of the Colorado River on a projecting rock cliff, now called Gold Point. Treasure seekers believe Barataria Island (now called Grand Terre) and Galveston Island are also likely spots for hidden caches.

The locations of Laffite's buried treasures remain a mystery. But it is known with certainty that he was a very wealthy man, and he did not take all his riches with him when he left Galveston Island in 1820. Most historians agree that he buried much of his treasure and personally marked and recorded the locations. But those secrets apparently died with Laffite.

Today he's called "the pirate of the Gulf Coast," although Laffite would undoubtedly have preferred to be called "privateer." No matter what you call him, his legend endures, and the search for his treasure continues from the Florida Keys to the mouth of the Rio Grande River.

Inca Gold

The Spaniard Francisco Pizarro and his small force of soldiers and horses first entered the Incan Empire of what is now Peru and Ecuador in 1532. Atahualpa, the king and major symbol of the Incan culture and religion, welcomed the Europeans with open arms to his capital city of Cuzco. It was the biggest mistake of his life—and the beginning of the end for his people.

The Spaniards were dumbstruck by the huge amount of solid gold the Incas used purely as decoration in their sacred temples and throughout the city. The gold was valued by the Incan civilization solely for its beauty and ornamental uses, not for financial purposes, since the Incas did not have any form of money in their society.

The Spaniards saw the gold as a precious substance that would make them and Spain wealthy beyond their wildest imagination. Solid gold plates, urns, vases, and figures were everywhere, some of them more than a hundred pounds in weight.

All Pizarro cared about was the gold, and in the course of obtaining it, he was perfectly willing to shed the blood of the hospitable, unsuspecting Incas. Without warning, Pizarro turned on Atahualpa and imprisoned him in his own palace. By seizing their leader, the Spaniard held the entire Incan Empire hostage.

Realizing the Spaniards' all-consuming desire for gold, Atahualpa made Pizarro a proposition that he couldn't refuse.

"I will cover this entire room with gold if you will set me free," he declared.

Pizarro was somewhat amazed by the Inca's offer. Mistaking his silence for dissatisfaction, Atahualpa reached to a point high on the wall and proclaimed, "My people will help me fill the room here with gold if you will set me free."

Pizarro accepted the offer and had the agreement written up in an official contract. The room was twenty-two feet long and seventeen feet wide, and the point the king had indicated on the wall was nine feet from the floor.

At once the word went out across the kingdom to bring gold to obtain freedom for their leader. Days passed and people brought gold plates, rings, bracelets, necklaces, statues, emblems, and ornaments into the room. The pile grew and grew until at last the great room was filled to the line with pure gold.

But Pizarro was greedy. He wanted even more gold. The desperate Atahualpa gave him directions to the city of Pachacamac, where there was even more of the "yellow metal." Instead of setting free the

king of the Incas as promised, Pizarro had the trusting leader taken out and strangled to death.

Word immediately spread throughout the Incan Empire that Pizarro had killed Atahualpa. The Incas were horrified and at once began to hide their gold from the crazed Spaniard.

Pizarro set out for Pachacamac in 1533, hoping to find more gold. But the Spaniard was too late and found nothing. The fortune in gold had been hidden from him.

It took over a month for Pizarro's men to melt down Atahualpa's ransom into bricks of gold. It's been estimated that more than $30 million worth of gold was sent back to Spain. In the sixteenth century, this wealth helped make that country the richest and most powerful in the world. Pizarro was a hero in Spain, the conqueror of the Incas. But he never found the gold of Pachacamac or the mines that were the source of the gold. He died in 1541, a disappointed man.

Where are the lost Incan mines and the hidden treasures of gold? Most are believed to be stored in burial places and caves high up in the Andes Mountains of Peru and Ecuador. Supposedly the treasure of Pachacamac is buried in one of the royal tombs, which was sealed and carefully concealed, as were the entrances to the mines. The secret of their locations was presumed to be known only by special priests, who passed the information from one generation of priests to the next.

One of the specific Incan treasures was the chain of Prince Huascar. It was seven hundred feet of pure gold, and each link in the chain measured five to seven inches in diameter. The chain was said to be so heavy that two hundred men were required to carry it!

In the early seventeenth century, a Spaniard named Valverde supposedly married an Indian woman who turned out to be an Incan princess. She showed him an incredible treasure cave high in the Andes, and they carried off a small portion of its contents, which made Valverde a very wealthy man.

The Spaniard made an accurate map so he could find his way back to the cave in case he wanted to return alone. According to his map, after traveling quite a long distance, Valverde eventually came to a crater of an extinct volcano. In the center of this bowl-shaped valley was a glacial lake and three snow-topped mountain peaks that rose above the crater. Crossing the crater, he came to an arched opening in the mountainside that led to the great treasure cavern.

In his will, Valverde left his map to the king of Spain, who was so impressed by the details it contained that he ordered an expedition to find the Incan treasure. For much of the route there was no difficulty with directions. But once the expedition came to a mountain called Margasitas, the Spaniards became confused and were forced to turn back. Other searchers followed the map, and all abandoned their quest—either because of the terrible cold and hardships of the trip or because they could never find the route beyond the peak of Margasitas.

In 1857, English botanist Richard Spruce followed Valverde's map, and he too became confused at Margasitas and gave up the quest. In the early twentieth century, an American colonel named E. C. Brooks got farther than any previous treasure hunter. He discovered the way past Margasitas and found the crater and glacial lake described by Valverde. But then a sudden and unexpected mountain storm flooded the crater and Brooks had to turn back, lucky to escape with his life. Although eager to return for another try, he became ill and died soon after.

There have been other Incan treasure expeditions. In 1929, one group reported the discovery of a cave containing an ancient Incan idol and several skeletons. A treasure hunter named Eric Loch was said to have discovered a new gold source, not linked to the Incan treasure, in the late 1930s. It was located near Mount Cerro Hermoso at an altitude of close to 20,000 feet in the Llanganates range of the Andes.

Do the Incan treasure and gold mines really exist? Most people think so, since the $30 million ransom for Atahualpa was only a very small portion of what was available throughout the Incan Empire.

Will it ever be found? The high altitude, thin air, and intense cold of the Andes Mountains are severe obstacles, and considering the geological changes in the landscape over the years, Valverde's detailed map may now be inaccurate and more confusing than ever.

Should the treasure of the Incas be sought after and found? Newly discovered Incan artifacts would only add to our knowledge about this unique people and their culture. But gold does strange things to people. Perhaps the untold wealth of the Incan Empire, high up in the Andes Mountains, should continue to lie untouched and hidden forever.

The Last Voyage of the *Juno*

Almost from the moment the thirty-four-gun frigate *Juno* left the Mexican port of Vera Cruz on January 15, 1802, she encountered one problem after another. Heavy storms raged throughout the Gulf of Mexico, and the high winds and rough seas took their toll on the *Juno* and her sister ship, the *Anfitrite*. The *Juno* lost a mast, and the *Anfitrite*'s sails and rigging were ripped and shredded by the storm.

"We have no choice," declared Captain Don Juan Ignacio Bustillo of the *Juno*. "We must head for San Juan, Puerto Rico, for repairs before we dare to cross the Atlantic to return home." Both ships were loaded with treasure and bound for Cádiz in Spain. *Juno* was carrying 300,000 pesos of silver (about $50,000).

Soon after reaching San Juan, the *Juno* and *Anfitrite* were ordered to wait for a troop transport, which was scheduled to be arriving from Africa. The two ships would provide transportation home to

Spain for the soldiers, many of whom were traveling with their wives and children. This route, from Africa to the Caribbean to Spain, was often used to avoid the strong currents and headwinds that ran southward along the African coast. It was a longer, less direct journey, but it was considered safer.

Finally, on October 1, the newly repaired ships set sail from Puerto Rico crowded with hundreds of passengers and loaded with treasure from Spain's New World colonies. But again they encountered bad weather. A week out of San Juan, somewhere south of Bermuda, the ships became separated, and the *Juno* headed north up the American coast in search of better weather. What she found was nothing but stormy seas and northeast winds.

"Captain, we've sprung a leak," reported the watch officer. "There are several feet of water in the hole!"

"If we have to work day and night, we must secure the ship and plug that leak," declared the captain.

But more bad luck followed. The wind gusted so strongly that it carried away the mainsail and forward topsail. A huge and powerful wave tore the *Juno*'s small launch from its frame, creating another hole in the hull.

It was now October 23. There was a lull in the storm, and Captain Bustillo examined both holes to determine which was the worst. "I want caulking stuffed between the seams," Bustillo ordered his crewmen. "Throw all artillery and the number three and four anchors overboard. Move all heavy equipment to the stern. We need to lift the bow to save the ship!"

"The caulking's not slowing the inflow of seawater, Captain," reported an exhausted officer.

"Then try hemp fiber, then mortar, then tar. Wrap

sails on the outside of the hull," Bustillo declared. "We have to slow the leak before the rising water sinks us completely!"

The *Juno*'s distress flag was up, and on October 24, the American schooner *Favorite* headed for the stricken ship. In case *Juno* had to be abandoned, the *Favorite* agreed to stand by and pick up her passengers and crew.

Captain Bustillo decided to head to a nearby port on the American coast with *Favorite* as an escort. But on October 27 *Juno* lost her rudder and her ability to steer in any direction. An oar was rigged to replace the rudder, and soldiers and crew began using buckets to bail out the rising water.

The wind grew in intensity that evening and changed directions. *Favorite* lost its mainsail, and the schooner's speed was drastically reduced, but both ships continued heading for the coast.

The storm worsened and the *Juno* was dangerously low in the water. *Favorite* tried to approach the sinking ship, but the heavy wind and rough seas prevented the American ship from closing the distance. Visibility was so poor that the *Favorite* couldn't see the *Juno* in the storm. But above the shrieking of the wind, the schooner's crew could hear cries for help, sounds that would haunt them the rest of their lives.

When dawn finally came on the morning of October 28, the *Favorite* searched the area but found no sign of the *Juno* or its passengers. The sea had completely and utterly swallowed up the Spanish ship! *Favorite* headed for Boston and reported the sinking on November 1, 1802.

All told, 425 people died that night. The captain believed they were closer to the coast than they actually were, but it was the strong winds of the storm that kept them far offshore.

The *Juno*'s last position was taken about twelve hours before the ship went down. She was several hundred miles off the coast of Cape May, New Jersey, east of Delaware Bay.

And what of the treasure the *Juno* carried? It lies together with the men, women, and children who went down with the ship anywhere from a few miles offshore to several hundred miles from the coast. Some even theorize it could be near the edge of the continental shelf in relatively shallow water.

The Last Stand and the Lost Gold

"Sir," said the soldier excitedly after saluting, "we've located the Indian encampment on the Little Bighorn. I don't think they have any idea we're here."

General George Armstrong Custer listened intently to his scout's report. Then he made a decision that would thereafter effect his place in history for all time.

"Surprise is on our side, gentlemen," declared Custer. "Major Reno, Captain Benteen—each of you take one third of the men in the regiment and move upstream. I'll lead the remaining third in a direct charge on the camp. When they try to escape upriver, both of you attack, and we'll overwhelm them. I'll give you two hours to get into position before the charge."

Custer had no idea that his forces were completely outnumbered, because the Indians had hidden most of their warriors in the nearby ravine. In addition, Custer was unaware that they had recently captured a new shipment of repeating rifles and outgunned his cavalry two to one.

It was June of 1876. Commanding General Alfred H. Terry was in charge of putting down the Indian uprising in southern Montana and driving the Indians back to their reservations. In an unprecedented move, the Cheyenne had joined with the Sioux and were led by Sioux chiefs Sitting Bull and Crazy Horse.

Ever since 1874, when gold had been discovered in the Black Hills, which was sacred land to the Sioux, clashes between the Indians and the white settlers had grown in intensity. Now the Indians were on the warpath and no traveler was safe.

General Terry sent General Custer and his Seventh Cavalry ahead to locate the enemy while Terry and his men marched on to join the main column of troops under General John Gibbon.

Meanwhile, forty miles to the southeast, a man named Gil Longworth was driving a mule-drawn freight wagon filled with gold from Bozeman, Montana. He was on his way to Bismarck, North Dakota, with two armed guards and was worried about the hostile Indians.

At the same time, a supply boat captained by Grant Marsh was headed to the junction of the Bighorn and Little Bighorn rivers to meet with General Terry. Longworth happened to meet Marsh when he was anchored for the evening and begged him to take the shipment of gold.

"The area's swarming with Sioux and Cheyenne," Longworth told Captain Marsh. "I'll never get this gold to Bismarck alive. Please take it with you," he pleaded.

Marsh finally agreed and took the gold. Later that night, he noticed that Indian campfires were visible everywhere in the area and decided to bury the shipment, whose weight slowed the boat down. Marsh; his first mate, Ben Thompson; and his engineer, a man named Foulk, went ashore and secretly hid the fortune in gold, presumably on the west bank of the Bighorn River, where he had earlier met Longworth.

Custer and his men, more than 230 in all, were eventually surrounded and massacred by the superior Indian force. The soldiers stood together, some on their knees, firing at the circling Indians. But the repeating rifles of the Sioux and Cheyenne warriors picked off soldier after soldier in rapid succession. When the dust had finally cleared, Custer, fourteen officers, and 233 soldiers lay dead. The men under Major Reno also suffered many casualties but were not completely wiped out. Captain Benteen, who had been ordered upstream by General Custer, arrived back in time to join Major Reno and his men in a defensive stand.

When Captain Marsh finally made contact with General Terry, his supply boat was used to carry Major Reno's casualties downriver to hospitals in Bismarck. The bullet-ridden bodies of Longworth, his two guards, and their burned-out freight wagon were eventually found several miles from the Little Bighorn.

The story of "Custer's Last Stand" swept through the country, and public outrage resulted in increased efforts to subdue and defeat the Indians. Three years later, in 1879, Marsh tried to trace the owners of the gold, but the freight company had gone out of business and all records of the prospectors who had mined the gold were missing.

Historians believe that neither Marsh, Thompson, nor Foulk made any attempt to retrieve the hidden gold. All continued working at their regular jobs on the river and none showed any signs of sudden wealth throughout their lifetimes.

Since these men were the only ones who knew the exact location, it is believed that the shipment is still buried somewhere on the banks of the Bighorn River about fifteen to twenty miles upstream from the junction of the Little Bighorn. It's most likely on the west bank, and probably not far from the river itself, since the three men hid the gold and returned to the boat in several hours' time.

So if you happen to visit the site of Custer's Last Stand, now an official United States National Monument, in Montana, think about that fortune in gold still buried somewhere along the Bighorn River. It's only a short drive from the place where Custer fell to the site where Captain Marsh might have buried the shipment.

Treasure seekers in the 1990s have one advantage and one disadvantage compared to their counterparts of the last century. They don't have to worry about hostile Indians, but they do need to get permission from whoever owns the land. Also, remember that—at today's market prices—the gold is now worth more than a million dollars!

Dream Treasure

With a sudden involuntary jerk of his body, Carney came awake instantly. He glanced at the clock. It was nearly time to get up for work. A moment later the dream came back to him in all its detail.

It was the second time in three days Carney had had this exact dream, and for that reason the experience was very disturbing to him. The last time he had had repeating dreams was as an eight-year-old child. In that dream an ugly, hairy man had chased him around his room but was never quite able to catch him. The current dream was comparatively harmless, but incredibly vivid.

As described by A. Hyatt Verrill in his book *They Found Gold! The Story of Successful Treasure Hunts*, Carney dreamed he was in Braden's Castle, an old stone house near Fort Myers on the Gulf Coast of Florida. It had been last used by war refugees many years before but now stood vacant and abandoned.

Carney saw a Spaniard dressed in old-fashioned clothes from the sixteenth or seventeenth century. Judging by the quality and cut of his garments, he appeared to be a Spanish nobleman or a gentleman of affluent means.

Carney watched as the Spaniard walked down a flight of stone stairs; after reaching the bottom, he lifted a stone slab and then proceeded to vanish into what appeared to be a secret underground chamber. Soon after, the Spaniard reappeared carrying a sack of gold coins. Looking straight at Carney, the older man declared, "All the rest is yours." Then he vanished into thin air like a ghost, and the dream ended.

At first Carney didn't think much of the dream. But when it repeated itself in its entirety—exactly as before—Carney was disturbed enough to mention it to a friend at lunch.

"Go see a psychic," his friend suggested. "They're able to interpret dreams. Maybe there's some symbolism they can help you with."

"Thanks for the suggestion, but I think I'll pass on that," replied Carney. "I don't need a fortune-teller to explain to me that in a past life I was a Spaniard who buried some treasure."

Carney laughed off the suggestion, but he secretly wondered whether the dream was really what it seemed to be, a message about a buried treasure. He would have forgotten about the entire incident, but then he had the same exact dream two more nights in a row.

Carney decided to visit Braden's Castle just to prove to himself that the dream was nothing more than an imaginative fantasy from his subconscious. "Maybe I saw a similar scene in an old Errol Flynn movie," he thought to himself. "I saw *Captain Blood* last week. Could that have triggered the dreams?"

Carney was somewhat apprehensive as he drove to Braden's Castle. He had never been there before in his life, but to his amazement, the stone house looked exactly as it had appeared in his dream. As Carney walked down the staircase—the very same stone stairway he had dreamed about—he thought that if he were to turn around quickly, he might see the ghost of the Spaniard standing there.

At the bottom of the stairs, Carney recognized the stone slab from the dream. His astonishment mixed with fear, and Carney felt dazed, as if he were moving in slow motion. He reached down and lifted the slab to reveal a very narrow set of stone stairs leading downward.

Using his flashlight, Carney stepped down slowly, stair by stair, until he was standing in a musty underground chamber. By now his heart was pounding so hard he wondered if he was going to faint. Shining the flashlight around the room, Carney saw chests and bags of gold and silver coins! "Am I dreaming?" he asked himself. "Is this really happening?"

It was definitely real, even though it was impossible to explain. Carney never revealed the exact amount of the treasure to anyone. He preferred to keep quiet about the details, but sometime later he gave his son enough money to buy his own business and live very comfortably himself.

How could he have dreamed of a treasure he didn't know about, in a place he had never visited? Why did the Spaniard's ghost choose Carney to receive the dream message of hidden treasure? Not even Carney can answer these questions.

A. Hyatt Verrill summed it up nicely when he wrote,

"Call it coincidence, telepathy, chance, spiritualism or what you will, it still remains an inexplicable mystery." Today, Carney is a happy and contented man who considers, accepts, and appreciates all the mysterious possibilities in life, both natural and supernatural.

Dungeon Rock

In Lynn, Massachusetts, it is said that the ghosts of Hiram and Edwin Marble haunt the treasure cave at Dungeon Rock. Many people who have visited the area at dusk have heard an eerie and consistent tapping from inside the cave. Most have fled in fear and panic. After all, the only thing worse than being alone in a haunted cave at dusk is being alone in a haunted cave in the dark of night!

Are there ghosts at Dungeon Rock? Does the cave contain a pirate's hidden treasure? Judge for yourself.

The story begins in the mid-seventeenth century. A pirate ship sailed near the mouth of the Saugus River, which borders the woods in which Dungeon Rock is located. Four men left the vessel and rowed up the river in a small boat, disappearing into the woods as the main ship sailed away.

Apparently, these men planned to live in the area for quite some time, since they asked the workers at the nearby iron foundry (now known as the Saugus Ironworks) to make them hatchets, shackles, and other tools and articles. When they paid for the work in silver coin, word spread in the area that pirates were living in Lynn Woods.

Within a few weeks, a British warship sailed up the river and armed soldiers set out to apprehend the men. Three of the four were captured, brought back to England, and stood trial for piracy. The fourth, a man named Thomas Veal, escaped his pursuers by hiding in Dungeon Rock cave, located under a rock ledge deep in the woods. Naturally, he took his treasure with him. Veal supposedly lived in the cave for more than a year, trading with locals for food and supplies.

But in the summer of 1658, New England was hit by a natural disaster of enormous proportions. There was an unusually large and violent earthquake. Veal was caught inside the cave when the rock ledge collapsed and large boulders sealed off the entrance, entombing him and his treasure forever.

Two hundred years passed. In the mid-nineteenth century, a man named Hiram Marble of the nearby town of Marblehead, Massachusetts, claimed that a local psychic had communicated with the spirit of Thomas Veal and related to him the exact whereabouts of the pirate's lost treasure. Although other treasure seekers had attempted to break through the cave's entrance, none had been successful.

Marble was so convinced of the treasure's location that in 1852 he purchased the land that included Dungeon Rock and the surrounding area. He used sledgehammers, crowbars, shovels, and explosives to get through the thick layer of rock that blocked the cave's entrance and filled up its interior.

Ten years later, he had tunneled through 135 feet of hard rock, chiseling out stairs that were seven feet high by six feet wide. The rock chips from the cave were piled nearby, eventually reaching a height of several hundred feet and a width of forty feet.

After sixteen years of what amounted to hard labor in search of Veal's elusive treasure, Hiram Marble died on November 10, 1868. Without missing a beat, his son, Edwin, who had been helping his father for years, continued to tunnel into the cave for twelve more years until his death in 1880.

What did the Marbles have to show for their twenty-eight years of hard labor? Absolutely nothing. They used up all their savings. Their health deteriorated from working all day in the damp cave. Yet every time they struck that sledgehammer against the rocks, each time they removed another large boulder, and whenever they chiseled, chipped, or blasted their way through more dirt and debris, both Hiram and Edwin firmly believed they would uncover the skeletal remains of Thomas Veal and a large chest of treasure valuable beyond their wildest imaginations.

What remains today of the Marbles' obsession is a man-made cave more than two hundred feet long and a pile of rock chips over two hundred feet high.

Does the treasure of Thomas Veal really exist? Were the Marbles only a few feet shy of their goal, or was it all just a crazy and useless quest? No one knows.

Today, the entrance to the cave at Dungeon Rock is blocked off by a large iron gate. According to author Robert Cahill, in his book *Pirates and Lost Treasure*: "There are many who still believe that by digging a few more feet, they might break into Veal's cave and find his treasure." For the Marbles, just a few more feet turned into twenty-eight years of backbreaking work.

And what about the tapping from inside the cave that many locals still claim to hear? "The ghosts of the Marbles," says Cahill, "still at work in the treasure cave at Dungeon Rock!"

Confederate Treasure

Things looked grim for the Confederate States of America (CSA) in early April 1865. Southern military defeats came one after another as Union troops pushed deep into the heart of Dixie. With the surrender of General Robert E. Lee at Appomattox Courthouse, Virginia, on April 9, the Civil War ended. The North was victorious and the Union was preserved.

In those last days of the conflict, those who had managed to safely keep gold, silver, and other valuables all over the South now rushed to hide or bury whatever they could to prevent it from falling into Union hands.

In the years since, a number of Civil War treasures have been unearthed in the South. One of the largest was discovered by Gayus Whitfield near Demopolis, Alabama, in June 1926. Whitfield located more than $200,000 in buried gold after going through some old papers his father had left to him. The papers contained directions for finding the gold, but for many years no one had bothered to see if the treasure was authentic. The cache of gold coins consisted mainly of twenty-dollar gold pieces minted in 1850.

Also in 1926, two young men were planting tobacco in Stewart County, Tennessee, when they found an old five-dollar piece in the dirt. In the next row of tobacco plants, the two brothers, Ernest and Austin Roberts, discovered a twenty-dollar gold piece. Before they were through, the two had unearthed $1,000 worth of gold coins. The money apparently had come from a glass jug that had been buried in the ground and somehow had broken, scattering its contents in the field.

In 1942, four children in Florence, Alabama, by chance uncovered a pot containing almost $6,000 worth of gold coins from Civil War days. It's hard to tell how many more similar incidents regarding the unearthing of buried treasure have occurred in the South. Many people likely kept quiet about their discoveries. By keeping a low profile, they avoided unwanted publicity and disputes and claims regarding the ownership of the treasure.

It's believed that the largest Civil War treasure has never been found. A huge British loan to the Confederate States was made in the last days of the war. Supposedly, more than $10 million in gold and silver was buried somewhere in Virginia. Others think this British gold may lie on the ocean floor in a shipwreck near Bermuda or the Bahamas, the victim of the Union navy's tight blockade of Southern ports.

Still another Confederate treasure has yet to be discovered and is described by Arnold Madison in his book *Lost Treasures of America*. Jefferson Davis, president of the CSA, fled from Richmond, Virginia, in the last days of the war with what was left of the South's treasury, about $500,000 in gold and silver, as well as his personal papers and official CSA documents.

Trying to outrun the federal troops, Davis and the treasure moved farther south. The gold and silver were eventually divided. Some of it was used to pay the troops, a portion was shipped out of the country, and another chunk went to Richmond bank agents.

About $35,000, along with CSA government documents and Davis's personal papers, was to be moved to Florida by wagon train. Davis went his own way, attempting to reach Texas to form a new Confederate government, but was finally captured by federal troops.

News of Davis's arrest reached the treasure train one week later. According to Madison, Captain Micajah Clark, realizing that the Confederate cause was lost, split up the money with his troops. One of the young soldiers, Tench Tilghman, supposedly buried his portion of the treasure, as well as Davis's personal papers and government documents. Madison believes the other men also buried their portions of the treasure, since they were eventually searched by federal troops and had no money in their possession.

The only hint as to the location of the treasure was from Tilghman's personal diary, which stated that the wagon train had camped in Florida "on the line of the Cedar Keys railroad in a forest northwest of Gainesville near a large plantation."

Madison notes that two years later, in 1867, Tilghman told a fraternity brother at a convention in New York City that he alone buried the treasure and it still lay undisturbed. A few days later, Tilghman died of a lung hemorrhage, never having revealed the exact location of the treasure site to anyone.

It is believed that the treasure and documents still lie somewhere near Gainesville, Florida. Today, the personal papers of Jefferson Davis and never-before-seen Confederate documents may be far more valuable than any amount of gold that might be discovered. Perhaps someday this special treasure will be found, lending more insight into and understanding of the turbulent times of a country nearly torn apart by the bloodiest conflict in American history.

Millions or Mud?

"Gentlemen," declared Don Manuel de Velasco, general of the Spanish fleet, to his council of war in 1702. "As you know, Spain and France are now in a state of war with England and her ally, the Netherlands. I have received a report that British and Dutch ships have already been sighted off Cádiz, our destination."

The Marquis de Chateaurenault, commander of the French warships that were escorting the treasure fleet back to Spain, remarked, "We cannot allow our treasure-laden galleons to fall into British hands. These ships are carrying three years' worth of New World gold, silver, and jewels. I propose sailing to Brest or La Rochelle in France to deceive the enemy."

"I cannot approve of that," replied Velasco. "My orders are to deliver these ships to King Philip V of

Spain, not to Louis XIV of France, even if he is Philip's grandfather!"

A compromise was finally reached. The twenty-three Spanish galleons and seventeen French vessels would head for the Bay of Vigo in Galicia, Spain, where the galleons would be safe in San Simon Bay, past the Strait of Rande. The hills overlooking the strait were protected by two well-manned forts, militiamen, and cannon.

For added protection, a log-and-chain boom was stretched across the opening of the narrow strait. The French warships were positioned inside the boom, ready to defend the Spanish galleons anchored behind them.

But instead of the treasure's being unloaded from the ships and sent inland immediately, everything soon came to a halt. Authorities in Cádiz opposed to the move said it was their right to unload the fleet. After some delay, the court in Madrid ordered that gold and silver coins and ingots intended for the royal treasury were to be shipped overland. Thousands of carts pulled by oxen were used to carry the treasure that came off the ships, but supposedly only about one tenth of the total cargo was transferred. Most of the treasure remained on board the galleons.

British Admiral Sir George Rooke, in charge of a force of two hundred ships and thousands of men, received a tip that the treasure galleons were at Vigo and headed there immediately. Rooke's fleet anchored outside the bay, and British and Dutch troops, supported by heavy artillery, attacked and overcame the Spanish and French militia in the forts.

At the same time, a squadron of heavy British vessels, driven by a strong wind, smashed through the log-and-chain defense, and with the rest of the fleet behind them, engaged Chateaurenault's French warships.

Velasco knew that the battle was lost. The French ships were no match for Rooke's men-of-war. They were outnumbered and outgunned. Decks were ablaze and masts fell as the British and Dutch cannons swept over the French ships.

"There is no escape for us," thought Velasco. "Scuttle the ships," he ordered his men. "Set fires above decks. Jettison whatever cargo you can. Open all hatches and portholes. Then save yourselves."

Within minutes, the galleons were in flames and some were sinking quickly. Rooke had scored a decisive victory, but was frustrated that he could not obtain the Spanish treasure.

"Save as many galleons as you can," he ordered, but it was too late for most of the treasure ships. The British managed to capture seven French vessels and six Spanish galleons, but seventeen treasure ships and twelve warships sank to the bottom of Vigo Bay.

On the way back to England, the largest Spanish prize, captured by the H.M.S. *Monmouth*, ran aground on a reef near Vigo and sank with millions of dollars' worth of treasure aboard. Several galleons supposedly reached England, with a combined treasure totaling about a million and a half pounds sterling in silver as well as gold.

Two main questions remain about the Vigo Bay treasure—Why hasn't it been salvaged? and How much was actually unloaded before the galleons were scuttled?

The ships burned and sank in fifty to seventy-five feet of water, and salvage operations by Spain and France began immediately after the British left. But between the lack of special diving equipment and the excessive mud of Vigo Bay, recovery of the treasure was next to impossible.

Since 1702, more than fifty salvage attempts have been made to retrieve the treasure, most of them unsuccessful. In 1728, Alexander Goubert, a Frenchman, was able to bring one ship to the surface, but it turned out to be a French warship and not a Spanish treasure galleon. In 1748, a Spaniard named Juan Antonio Rivero tried for the second time to salvage some portion of the treasure, and this time he recovered about 200,000 pieces of silver.

A Welshman named William Evans brought up plates of silver in 1760 using a diving bell apparatus. In 1829, an Englishman named Isaac Dickson salvaged silver plates, coins, and ingots. The Magen-Berthe team tried out some new diving equipment in 1869 and managed to bring up five heavy silver plates from the muddy ocean floor.

In the early twentieth century, Jose Pino and Carlos Iberti used an invention called the hydroscope that allowed people on the surface to observe the sea floor through a telescopic tube. Many items were salvaged by Pino, and he also discovered and charted the location of most of the wrecks. He raised a galleon to the surface on two different occasions, but they both broke apart because of heavy mud deposits and fell back to the bottom of Vigo Bay. Iberti estimated that Pino successfully salvaged about 20 percent of the total treasure.

The most recent treasure-hunting operation took place in 1958 and was led by an American engineer named John S. Potter. Potter believed he had discovered the wreck captured by the *Monmouth*, the richest treasure ship in the fleet. The shifting seabed and thirty-foot-plus layer of mud and ooze caused the Potter team to eventually abandon its search.

Estimates of the value of the Vigo Bay treasure have ranged from $37 million to $140 million. Although some of the treasure has been recovered, most is still believed to be buried where it sank over 275 years ago. Or is it?

With so many salvage operations undertaken over the years, even by the laws of chance, one would think someone would have eventually come across a large portion of the treasure. Perhaps more of the treasure was unloaded than was first thought. Yet certain Spanish documents have revealed that very little of the unloaded treasure reached the king in Madrid, and it is believed that much of it was stolen or buried ashore.

There are those who think most of the gold and silver was already unloaded before Sir George Rooke attacked the French warships in Vigo Bay. A portion of the treasure obviously remained on the sea floor, or Spanish and French divers wouldn't have immediately started salvage operations.

Does Vigo Bay hold the richest of all sunken treasures? Many believe it does.

How much of the treasure actually remains on the ocean floor? Some think the only riches at the bottom of Vigo Bay are the huge amounts of money so many people have sunk into treasure-hunting expeditions that have ended in disappointment and failure. Perhaps one day the truth will be known.

Glossary

AFFLUENT: wealthy.

ALLY: friend, supporter.

ALMIRANTA: Spanish galleon carrying the second in command of a convoy.

AMPUTATE: cut off.

BARON: a nobleman.

BELEAGUERED: under siege, surrounded.

BENEFICIARY: person named to receive income or inheritance in case of the owner's death.

BISON: four-legged mammal; the American buffalo.

BOOM: chain or cable that obstructs navigation.

BULLION: gold or silver in the form of bars or ingots.

BUOYED: marked a spot with a floating object.

CACHE: something stored or hidden.

CAPITANA: Spanish galleon carrying the commanding officer of a convoy.

CAULKING: material used to stop up cracks or leaks.

CAVALRY: combat troops on horseback.

CHALICE: cup, goblet.

CIRCUMNAVIGATE: sail around the earth.

COHORT: friend, partner.

CONFISCATE: seize, grab.

CONVOY: fleet, procession.

CUTLASS: short, heavy, curved sword.

DECAPITATE: cut off the head of.

DECIPHER: decode, make understandable.

DOUBLOONS: Spanish gold coins.

DREDGE: machine that scoops up earth and materials from a river or sea bottom.

ELUSIVE: slippery, able to escape detection.

EXTINCT: no longer in existence.

FOUNDRY: establishment for melting and molding metals.

FRIGATE: sailing warship designed for high speed.

GALLEON: large, heavy, Spanish sailing vessel with several decks.

GILDED: coated with gold.

GOBIERNO: Spanish war galleon often carrying the highest-ranking military man in a convoy.

GOBLET: drinking container.

HEMORRHAGE: burst or ruptured blood vessel.

HEMP FIBER: used to make rope.

INFESTED: overrun, invaded.

INGOTS: a mass of metal cast into a convenient shape (often a bar) for storage or transportation.

JETTISON: throw overboard.

KILN: furnace or oven.

MAST: upright pole that supports sails on a vessel.

MATCHLOCK PISTOL: handgun ignited by a slow match.

MORTAR: mixture of sand and lime, like plaster or cement.

PANORAMIC: unlimited view in all directions.

PILLAGE: steal, assault; see *plunder*.

PLUNDER: take by force; see *pillage*.

POWDER MAGAZINE: compartment for the storage of ammunition and explosives.

PRIVATEER: privately owned ship hired to attack and plunder enemy ships; a sailor on such a ship.

PROSPECTOR: someone who searches for gold and other precious metals.

PSYCHIC: a person who is sensitive to supernatural forces.

REFUGEE: one who flees home for safety in time of war or disaster.

RELIC: object from the past.

RUDDER: steering device on a ship.

SALVAGE: goods, treasure, or property rescued from a shipwreck.

SCHOONER: ship with two or more masts.

SCUTTLE: open holes and hatches on a ship to sink it.

SLUDGE: mud, filth.

SUPPRESS: overpower.

THICKET: thick, dense growth of shrubs or bushes.

TRANQUIL: calm, peaceful.

TREK: journey, trip.

URN: type of vase or container.

VEIN: a defined body of ore in rock.

Bibliography

Blassingame, Wyatt. *Diving for Treasure.* Philadelphia: Macrae-Smith Company, 1971.

Cahill, Robert Ellis. *Pirates and Lost Treasures.* Peabody, Mass.: Chandler-Smith Publishing House, Inc., 1987.

Cochran, Hamilton. *Freebooters of the Red Sea.* New York: The Bobbs-Merrill Company, Inc., 1965.

Coffman, F. L. *1001 Lost, Buried or Sunken Treasures.* New York: Thomas Nelson and Sons, 1957.

Daly, Robert. *Treasure.* New York: Random House, 1977.

DeLatil, Pierre, and Jean Rivoire. *Sunken Treasure.* New York: Hill and Wang, 1962.

Dobie, J. Frank. *Coronado's Children.* New York: The Literary Guild of America, 1931.

Driscoll, Charles B. *Pirates Ahoy!* New York: Farrar and Rinehart, 1941.

Ferguson, Robert G. *Guidebook to Lost Western*

Treasure. Los Angeles: The Ward Ritchie Press, 1973.

Groushko, Mike. *Treasure.* Philadelphia: Courage Books, 1990.

Hancock, Ralph, and Julian A. Weston. *The Lost Treasure of Cocos Island.* New York: Thomas Nelson and Sons, 1960.

Haydock, Tim. *Treasure Trove.* New York: Henry Holt and Company, 1986.

Horner, Dave. *The Treasure Galleons.* New York: Dodd, Mead and Company, 1971.

Lovelace, Leland. *Lost Mines and Hidden Treasure.* San Antonio, Tex.: The Naylor Company, 1956.

Madison, Arnold. *Lost Treasures of America.* New York: Rand McNally and Company, 1977.

McDonald, Douglas. *Nevada: Lost Mines and Buried Treasures.* Las Vegas, Nev.: Nevada Publications, 1981.

Mitchell, John D. *Lost Mines of the Southwest.* Glorieta, N.M.: The Rio Grande Press, Inc., 1979 (originally published in 1933).

Nesmith, Robert I. *Dig for Pirate Treasure.* New York: The Devin-Adair Company, 1958.

Perrin, Rosemarie D. *Explorers Ltd. Guide to Lost Treasure in the United States and Canada.* Harrisburg, Pa.: Cameron House, Stackpole Books, 1977.

Swinburne, Laurence, and Irene Swinburne. *Mysterious Buried Treasures.* New York: Contemporary Perspectives, Inc., 1979.

Time-Life Books editors. *Lost Treasure.* Alexandria, Va.: Time-Life Books, 1991.

Tompkins, B. A., ed. *Treasure.* New York: Times Books, 1979.

Verrill, A. Hyatt. *They Found Gold! The Story of*

Successful Treasure Hunts. Glorieta, N.M.: The Rio Grande Press, Inc., 1972.

Von Mueller, Karl. *Encyclopedia of Buried Treasure Hunting.* Weeping Water, Neb.: Exanimo Press, 1965.

Weight, Harold O. *Lost Mines of Death Valley.* Twentynine Palms, Calif.: The Calico Press, 1961.

Wilkins, Harold T. *Treasure Hunting.* Glorieta, N.M.: The Rio Grande Press, Inc., 1939, 1973.

Wilson, Ian. *Undiscovered.* New York: Beech Tree Books-William Morrow, 1987.

GHOSTS, HAUNTINGS and MYSTERIOUS HAPPENINGS

The Whaley House

It's been called one of the most actively haunted houses in the world. The U.S. Chamber of Commerce and the State of California have officially recognized the Whaley House as a genuine haunted house!

Located in Old Town San Diego, the two-story mansion was built in 1856 by city pioneer Thomas Whaley. In addition to being the residence of the Whaley family, parts of the house were also used at various times as a county courthouse, a church, a post office, a public school, and home base for a theater group.

The last Whaley to live in the house was Lillian, who died in 1953 at the age of eighty-nine. Today, the house has been preserved as a historical museum and is open to the public.

Strange, unexplained incidents began happening in 1960. These were noted in detail by Jean Reading, the curator and chief historian of the Whaley House.

Footsteps, piano music, and rapping noises have been heard. Visitors have seen strange lights and moving objects. Some people have smelled strong odors of perfume or cigar smoke. Others have felt cold spots or mysterious touches. A number of people claim even to have seen actual ghosts!

One person reported seeing the figure of a small woman in a long hoop skirt. Another saw a man in old-fashioned dress. A ghost dog has been spotted from time to time, and the noises of a baby crying have been heard.

In the 1980s a young woman who worked as a tour guide at the Whaley House told everyone she wanted to see a real ghost.

"Be patient, Denise," said Jean Reading. "It can be dangerous saying things like that out loud in a house like this. The walls have ears," she added.

One Christmas, some visitors to the mansion heard the sound of footsteps. Jean and Denise went upstairs to investigate the vacant second floor.

In the main bedroom, the women discovered two windows wide open. I'm sure these were shut, thought Jean. Apparently, the horizontal bolts on the windows had been pulled back by unseen hands!

As they walked over to check on the nursery, a man's voice suddenly boomed out with laughter. Denise grew pale as she turned toward Jean, who stood frozen, unable to move a muscle.

Finally, Denise whispered, "Let's get out of here!" Both women bolted down the stairs.

Did they hear the laughter of Thomas Whaley? Maybe so, but the exact place where the mysterious event occurred was above the location of an old execution site. A man named Yankee Jim Robinson was hanged at that very spot on which the Whaley House was built!

If ever there was a restless and angry spirit, Jim Robinson was one. He had been arrested for stealing a boat and was sentenced to hang by a drunken judge. Jim didn't believe they would go through with the execution because it was much too harsh a sentence for the crime of theft. He thought it would be called off at the last second, but unfortunately, it wasn't.

To add insult to injury, Yankee Jim didn't die instantly of a broken neck, as do most victims of hanging. He dropped only a few feet and hung there for thirty to forty seconds before he finally strangled to death.

Some say the heavy footsteps heard in the **Whaley House are those of the ghost of Yankee Jim Robinson.**

The spirit of Thomas Whaley is also restless. When he was alive, part of his home was used as the county courthouse, and Whaley was paid sixty-five dollars a month for the privilege. The county records were stored there for several years.

But as time went by, large portions of the population of Old Town shifted to a new area, called New Town. The people of New Town wanted the courthouse moved to their area, but Thomas Whaley refused. The people of Old Town supported Whaley and vowed to fight the citizens of New Town.

When Whaley was away on a business trip, his opponents came to the house at midnight and forced their way in. Holding Mrs. Whaley at gunpoint, they took the county records and left.

When he returned, Whaley was infuriated at what had happened! For nineteen years he tried to get the county to pay the remaining months on their lease and reimburse him for repairs on the building required after the break-in. But the case was never settled. Whaley died in 1890, angry and bitter over the injustice of his situation.

Other ghosts haunt the mansion. The small woman seen by many visitors is probably Thomas's wife, Anna, who was only 4 feet 11 inches tall. The crying baby is very likely the spirit of seventeen-month-old Tom Whaley, the son of Thomas and Anna, who died in an upstairs room of the house.

Many have seen and been frightened by these strange incidents at the Whaley house, but no one has ever been harmed or injured. This well-documented haunted house continues to attract visitors year round.

The Whaley House   140

Many have seen and been frightened by these
strange positions at the Whaley House, but no one
has ever been harmed or injured. The well-
documented haunted house continues to attract
visitors year round.

The Haunted Battlefield

"Such a beautiful and peaceful-looking place," said the Englishwoman. She had ridden a bicycle from her hotel to the Scottish Highlands to see the Pass of Killiecrankie.

It's hard to believe this was the site of so much blood, pain, and death, she thought to herself. Surrounded by high cliffs, she gazed at the narrow, rocky valley below her. It was a lovely day, and not a cloud was in the bright blue sky.

As the afternoon wore on, the woman recalled the history of the area. In 1689, there was a terrible battle in the pass between English soldiers and Scottish Highlanders. The English had removed the Scottish King, James II, from the throne and replaced him with Mary and her husband, William of Orange. Scotland still supported James. At Killiecrankie, the Scots won a total victory over the British, slaughtering the Redcoats to the last man. After the battle, the Highlanders stripped the bodies of all valuables and killed any wounded.

Killiecrankie was the only victory for the Highlanders, who were eventually overwhelmed by the British forces.

The woman sat down in front of a tree and looked all around her. Does the land see and remember? she thought. I wonder.

It was fall, and as the sun dropped in the sky, the woman felt a chill in the air. She was so relaxed she didn't feel like moving.

I've got plenty of food in my picnic basket and a heavy coat, she thought. I think I'll spend the night here and bicycle back to the hotel in the morning.

She leaned back against the tree, closed her eyes, and eventually fell asleep. Hours later, she woke with a start. Was that faraway thunder she heard, or the sound of guns?

The moon was so bright that she could see by her watch that it was 2 A.M. Suddenly, she heard noises erupt throughout the valley below her. She watched as an unbelievable scene unfolded.

A large group of red-coated soldiers and their horses and pack mules gathered below. They groped for their guns and seemed to be in total disorder. When the woman looked up, she saw the reason for their confusion.

Swarms of Highlanders, screaming the name of James II, descended on the Redcoats. The huge band of Scottish warriors carried swords and shields against the English flintlock guns and bayonets.

Shrieks and cries filled the air as the British were slaughtered. Their guns were no match for the Scottish fighters. Horses panicked and soldiers begged for mercy, but there was none. Men were butchered and the ground turned red with their blood.

The woman was horrified and couldn't speak. The battle was totally one-sided. Finally, unable to watch any longer, she sobbed and covered her eyes. Then a silence fell over the valley.

Moments later she looked up. Bodies and limbs were strewn everywhere. A few men, still alive, moaned in pain while others simply cried. The Englishwoman smelled the scent of death in the air.

Living people moved among the bodies. They pulled the clothes off corpses, taking shoes, belts, and buttons. A young woman scavenger, carrying a basket and a dagger, did her work not far from the Englishwoman. One soldier, barely alive, moved slightly as the woman tried to take his wedding ring. Without hesitation, she bent forward and slit his throat.

The Englishwoman cried out. The scavenger

turned, looked directly into her eyes, and began moving slowly toward her.

"No! No!" the Englishwoman screamed in her mind, but she was so frozen with fear that she could not speak. As the young woman with the dagger leaned close, the Englishwoman lost consciousness.

When she opened her eyes it was daylight. She was alone and cold. The Pass of Killiecrankie was beautiful and peaceful once again. There was no sign of the bloodshed she had witnessed. Shivering, she slowly pulled herself up, climbed on her bicycle, and rode back to the hotel. When she told the staff what had happened, they nodded their heads.

"Over the years, others have seen the awful things you saw," said the hotel owner. "The pass is haunted. Too many died terrible deaths there for the spirits to be at rest."

Others may say the Englishwoman just had a bad dream that seemed real. It's only natural that the battle was on her mind as she fell asleep under the tree.

But those who live near the site of this bloody battlefield believe the land was witness to so much death and destruction that it can never erase the pain and violence.

Do images of past battles replay themselves again and again? The Englishwoman thought so. Do you?

Rosemary Brown

The nineteenth-century composer and pianist Franz Liszt first came to Rosemary Brown when she was seven years old. At the time of the visit, however, he had been dead for more than fifty years!

According to Rosemary, Liszt declared, "When you grow up, I will come back and give you music."

Years later, beginning in 1964, Rosemary, who lives in England, began communicating with a group of famous composers from the past. In addition to Liszt, they included Chopin, Beethoven, Bach, Brahms, Schumann, Schubert, Debussy, Grieg, and Rachmaninoff.

These men supposedly dictated musical compositions to Rosemary, who wrote them down in manuscript form. Then, with the help of her spirit friends, she played them on the piano.

"She's doing it herself," stated many nonbelievers. The music was analyzed by experts. Rosemary took psychological tests, intelligence tests, and musical tests. People investigated her background, her friends, her neighbors, and her musical training.

They found that Rosemary was a normal person of medium intelligence with a very limited musical background. She had taken some piano lessons, but stopped after a while. Poor since childhood, she had spent most of her life trying to make ends meet.

"Communicate with dead composers? Impossible!" declared one musician. "Perhaps she had advanced musical training, and then an episode of amnesia which made her forget," he suggested. Rosemary's family doctor stated that that was nonsense.

As a child she did have many psychic experiences. She often saw the spirits of dead people and realized at a young age that she had special powers and abilities.

In 1969, the British Broadcasting Corporation (BBC) did a documentary on Rosemary and her music. As a test, she sat at a piano, with BBC staff present, and waited for Liszt to put in an appearance.

In a matter of minutes, Liszt was there, dictating.

a new piece. It was very difficult, with six sharps and different rhythms for the right and left hands. The completed manuscript was too hard for Rosemary herself to play. One of the BBC officials, who was an excellent pianist, was able to play it. He said, "Mrs. Brown, I think you've got something here!"

The piece was then analyzed by an expert on Franz Liszt. He stated that it was definitely characteristic of the great composer.

Rosemary has performed in a similar way with other composers who communicate with her. She sits at the piano and with great speed writes down what they dictate to her. Each completed piece is written in the exact style of that particular composer!

"Rosemary Brown is a gifted and talented musician," some experts say.

"Not true," replies Rosemary. "I am only the link to these great men. They dictate the music and I write it down."

How can it be proven that Rosemary is really in touch with the spirit world? For some, no amount of proof will ever be convincing. They are totally closed to the possibility.

But for other open-minded individuals, proof is possible. A Hungarian photographer named Tom Blau became a believer in 1970 when he was taking photos of Rosemary for the German magazine *Der Spiegel*. During the session, Rosemary admitted to the other journalists present that Liszt and her late mother were visible to her in the room.

Blau asked Liszt a question in German, a language Rosemary didn't understand. Rosemary said that Liszt nodded to her and answered, *"Ja,"* which means yes.

Then, according to Rosemary, Liszt said in English, "I'm going to fetch someone." He left the room. A few seconds later he returned. "He's back now," explained Rosemary to Blau and the other journalists, "and he's brought a woman with him." Rosemary went on to describe the woman in detail. "She's wearing a shawl and has very small feet," she added.

Blau's eyes widened. "You've just described my mother. I've always felt bad that I wasn't with her when she died," he said. "Now I feel better about it."

Later, Blau wrote to Rosemary: "I was moved and stirred by what occurred . . . You gave me a description so striking and convincing that I can't forget it."

How could Rosemary have known what Tom Blau's dead mother looked like? She had never met him before that day in 1970.

Did Rosemary really communicate with the famous composers of the past? Tom Blau thinks so.

Many believe Rosemary herself is the talent behind the music, not Liszt or Beethoven. Until there is more definite proof, the story of Rosemary Brown remains a strange, unsolved mystery.

A Mother's Warning

The American crew of the B-29 bomber was returning to their base in England during the last years of World War II. This long-range bomber was the largest and heaviest airplane of the war. Its payload of 20,000 pounds of bombs had been successfully dropped deep in the heart of enemy territory.

Most of the crew of twelve were asleep after the enemy raid. Only the pilot and copilot stayed awake to guide the B-29 home after the mission.

The night skies were clear of German fighter planes, but the pilots kept their eyes peeled for the enemy. If they were attacked, their thirteen machine guns and twenty-millimeter cannon could blow any speedy Messerschmitt fighter out of the sky.

The young tail gunner was sound asleep in his revolving turret at the rear of the big bomber. In his dream, he suddenly saw his mother. She was standing on the wingtip of the airplane, dressed in a long, white robe that blew in the wind.

"Mom," the young corpsman said in his dream, quite astonished. "What are you doing here? You died three years ago. You're not even alive!"

"Son, wake up," she called to him. "Danger is very near. Wake up. You must wake up!"

The young flyer stirred in his sleep. His mother's voice echoed in his brain: "Wake up, wake up." Suddenly, the tail gunner awoke with a start.

"Mom?" he whispered. He realized the image of his mother had only been a dream. But just then he spotted a German fighter plane flying right above the B-29. The pilots would never have seen it from where they were seated.

"Wake up, everyone!" the tail gunner screamed over his microphone. "Bandit at twelve o'clock high! He appears to be all alone. Rise and shine, boys. Let's give the German on our tail a big Army Air Corps welcome!"

Although the speedy Messerschmitt Me 109 had two cannons and two machine guns, the lone German pilot wasn't prepared for the firepower that suddenly knocked him out of the sky.

"This is a message from my mother," said the tail gunner as he fired burst after burst at the enemy plane, which fell to the earth in flames. If his

mother hadn't appeared in his dream to warn and wake him, the B-29 would have been a sitting duck!

Are there limits to a mother's love? Did this woman come back from the dead to warn her son of danger? Or was it just a coincidence that he dreamed of her at that exact moment?

The young tail gunner was convinced that his mother saved his life and the lives of the crew. How would you explain it?

The Ghosts of
West Point

"The Thayer place is haunted," declared the major. "Strange things happen here."

The year was 1972, and Ed and Lorraine Warren had been invited to speak to the cadets at West Point. The Warrens were "demonologists," experts on the supernatural and the occult.

The major was giving them a tour of the U.S. Military Academy. Their first stop had been the white-painted brick Thayer residence.

"It's named for Colonel Sylvanus Thayer, who was West Point superintendent from 1817 to 1833," the major explained. "Our current superintendent lives here now."

"People have seen some unusual things at the house," he continued. "The beds are mysteriously turned down, and when they are made up, some invisible force turns them down again."

He then led the Warrens into the kitchen. "See that wet spot on the bread board? Whenever we dry it, it keeps coming back over and over again. It's been that way for months!" the major said.

"The superintendent and his wife have seen things at night and so have their guests. Doors slam and clothes are torn and ripped out of drawers," he added.

Lorraine could feel evidence of the supernatural at the Thayer house. There were troublesome spirits in the air.

In one of the rooms, Lorraine sat in a rocking chair and detected the presence of former President John F. Kennedy. She mentioned this to the major.

"JFK stayed in this room when he visited West Point," the major replied.

In the master bedroom, Lorraine felt the angry spirit of a strong woman who always got her way, "a jealous, possessive spirit who felt the house belonged to her and resented anybody else who lived in it," Lorraine declared.

When Lorraine told the major, he said that General Douglas MacArthur's wife had also lived in the Thayer house at one time. She ran the place with an iron hand, and the servants were afraid of her.

"That explains why the beds were always turned

down and why the clothes were tossed around," said the major.

But Lorraine sensed something else in the house. She believed some violent act had happened in or been connected with the house in some way.

Later that evening, after the Warrens had addressed the cadets, they were preparing to leave West Point. Lorraine glanced out the window and saw a ghostly figure of a man looking up at her. He wore an old-fashioned uniform from the past with no braids or insignia of any kind. Somehow he was able to communicate with Lorraine.

"He said his name was Greer and he was not free," Lorraine told one of the military aides accompanying them. But the name was not familiar to the young aide.

A week later Lorraine received a phone call. It was the aide from the academy.

"Mrs. Warren, I did some research on that man named Greer," he told her. "He attended West Point around the turn of the century and murdered another man. But he was cleared by a military court and absolved of blame, so why is his spirit so troubled?"

"We'll never really know the answer," explained Lorraine. "Perhaps he can't accept what happened and is still angry at himself."

Once the officials of West Point knew who all the ghosts were, they became less frightened and even more intrigued by their ghostly companions!

Dandy

The boy and his sister knew that their dog, Dandy, was devoted to them. He was a large and powerful retriever, trained as a gun dog for hunting. Sometimes Dandy acted so smart he almost seemed human.

Boy and dog went everywhere together. The boy was an expert duck and bird hunter and bicycled for miles around the beautiful English countryside to pursue his favorite sport.

Up at dawn, the boy and his dog spent their days traveling over hills and through swamps and grasslands. Dandy swam through the water and ran across the marshlands and fields. He loved to retrieve game for his beloved master.

Arriving home, Dandy would run and play with

the boy's sister or sometimes just nap at her feet. He felt peaceful and contented as the familiar, loving hand stroked his muscular back.

As the years went by, the boy and girl grew up and began spending less and less time with Dandy. But the dog was still devoted to them. Whenever the young man came home, the dog would accompany the family to the train station.

When the train came in, Dandy would run back and forth across the platform. As soon as he recognized his master, he would jump up on his hind legs and grab the hat off the young man's head. Then Dandy would trot home next to the car, hat in mouth, while the neighbors looked on with amusement.

One day, Dandy didn't come to the train station to meet the young man. When the master got home, he found that his devoted dog was very sick and couldn't walk.

Dandy was dying. For weeks during the winter, he had been retrieving sticks in the river. Then, night after night, he was mistakenly shut in the stable by the caretaker, soaking wet and without food.

The young man was heartbroken to see his ill dog. He held him close, whispering words of love and comfort to his pet. Dandy died that night in his master's arms.

At the same time, the man's sister was in Lon-

don, fast asleep in her room. Suddenly she awoke as a large dog jumped onto her bed.

The young woman switched on a small lamp next to the bed and saw Dandy. "Dandy boy," she said with delight. "What are you doing here?" She reached out to hug him and he licked her cheek. As she started to close her arms around the big dog, she suddenly found that she was hugging nothing but empty space!

"Well of course he can't be here," she said to herself. "I must be dreaming."

The young woman looked at her clock to see what time it was. She tried to get back to sleep but was too restless and worried. Something must be wrong at home, she thought to herself.

The next morning the young woman contacted her brother. She discovered that Dandy had died during the night at the very same time he had appeared in her room!

"I smelled Dandy and felt his tongue on my cheek," she told her brother.

Did the spirit of Dandy come to see his beloved mistress one last time? Or was it just her imagination?

"He came to say good-bye to me," she declared as tears filled her eyes, "and I will never forget him!"

A Feeling of Dread

"My dear, I don't feel very well," said Senator Lewis Linn of Missouri to his wife. "Probably an attack of indigestion. Will you go to the dinner party tonight and explain my absence to our host?"

"You don't look well, Lewis," replied Mrs. Linn. "I don't want to leave you alone tonight."

"Don't worry, dear," he explained. "General Jones will see you safely to the party, and he'll come back and stay with me during the evening. It's all been arranged."

The year was 1840, and the Linns lived in Washington, D.C., during the presidency of Martin Van Buren. At the party, Mrs. Linn sat next to General Macomb and opposite Senator Wright of New York, a close friend of her husband.

Mrs. Linn worried throughout the party. She tried to shake the feeling that something was dreadfully wrong at home. After all, her husband wasn't alone. In the event of an emergency, General Jones would notify her immediately.

As the night wore on, Mrs. Linn's uneasiness grew with each passing moment. Eventually she felt she must return home right away!

"Whatever is the matter?" asked Senator Wright when he saw how preoccupied she was.

Mrs. Linn explained her urgent feelings. Seeing her so pale and upset, Senator Wright and his wife took their friend home immediately.

At the door he said, "I'll call on you tomorrow and we'll have a good laugh about all this. I'm certain Lewis is fine!"

Mrs. Linn said good night, then went inside the house and spoke to the landlady.

"How is my husband feeling?" she asked.

"Very well, madam," the landlady replied. "He took a bath and is probably sound asleep by now. General Jones left a half-hour ago."

Mrs. Linn hurried upstairs to her husband's bedroom. When she opened the door, a blast of thick, dark smoke suddenly brought her to her knees. She scrambled up and rushed into the room.

The bed pillows were on fire! The air from the open door fanned the flames, and the fire burned brighter. She saw her husband lying on the bed, unconscious and at the mercy of the smoke and flames.

When Mrs. Linn ran to the bed to try to smother the blaze, her dress caught fire! As the flames spread over her clothes, she threw herself into the large tub that was still filled with water from her husband's bath. The flames were doused.

Pulling herself out of the tub, Mrs. Linn grabbed the burning pillows and plunged them into the bath water. Then, using what was left of her strength, she dragged her unconscious husband off the bed and screamed for help.

Later Dr. Sewell, the family physician, examined Senator Linn. "The senator is suffering from severe smoke inhalation," the doctor explained. "Three more minutes in that smoke-filled room and he would have died. You're lucky to have come at the exact moment you did!"

Mrs. Linn suffered burns on her arm. It took three months for her husband to fully recover from the accident. When Senator Wright heard what had happened, he was speechless.

How could Mrs. Linn have known that her husband would be in danger? She experienced a premonition, which is a warning of disaster.

Certain individuals have a special ability that extends beyond the normal five senses. This is called extrasensory perception, or ESP. Today, the knowledge of certain events before they actually

happen is called precognition. This phenomenon cannot be easily explained, even though it has been experienced by many people.

Was Mrs. Linn's feeling of danger a simple coincidence, or was it real precognition?

The House on Plum Tree Lane

Harold Cameron was making a final inspection of the large mansion he had just rented. It was a twenty-minute drive outside of Philadelphia in the town of Wynne, Pennsylvania. The seventeen-room house dated back to revolutionary times and the grounds were beautifully landscaped.

It was the late 1940s and Harold needed a home for his family of seven. There was Harold's wife, Dorothy, his two college-age sons, Hal and Bob, ten-year-old Carrol, four-year-old Janet, and six-month-old Michael.

The Camerons had recently moved from the West Coast to the Philadelphia area. Harold had been chosen to open an office and warehouse there for the Aluminum Corporation of America.

What a bargain, thought Harold as he examined his family's new home. They planned to move in the next day. "Three floors, four fireplaces, a circular staircase, servants' quarters, and all for only $300 a month!" he commented.

He walked down the stairway into the basement. "I'll check out the furnace," he said, looking around. "Everything else seems fine."

After he inspected the furnace, Harold walked back upstairs. As he headed for the front door, he heard the door to the library creak open, followed by the sound of footsteps. "Who is it?" he asked.

There was no answer. The afternoon sun had set, and it was dark inside the house.

"Is that you, Bob? Hal, are you there?" he called, thinking it might be his sons. "Answer me, please."

Harold lit a match. He saw the library door. "I'm sure that door was closed when I came in," he thought.

Suddenly the match flickered out. Again he heard footsteps. They seemed to go up the stairs right next to where Harold stood.

It sounds like a woman wearing floppy slippers, Harold thought as he lit another match. The sound was so close he felt he could have reached out and grabbed the person going upstairs.

All of a sudden the spot where Harold stood became icy cold. He grew frightened. "Who is it?" he called again. "Dorothy, is that you?"

Harold heard the footsteps on the second floor

and then on the third floor. Without waiting for an explanation, he bolted out the front door and found his family waiting for him in the car! None of them had been in the house!

By the time the Camerons moved in the next day, Harold was beginning to think he had imagined the whole thing. But he hadn't!

Two weeks later, Harold heard the footsteps again. Then Dorothy and the rest of the family heard them. The sounds seemed to come from the library.

Over the next several months, the Camerons heard footsteps on the drive outside the house. This time, however, they were heavy steps, crunching the gravel from the coach house to the main house and up to the front door. Then the sounds stopped.

"It's a man's footsteps, Dad," said Hal. "A big man. The ones inside the house are a woman's steps."

During the Camerons' stay in the mansion, they experienced a variety of ghostly phenomena. A terrible smell would come and go in a small part of the bedroom at night, and doorknobs would mysteriously turn without being touched.

After being thoroughly frightened in the beginning, the Camerons remained strong and eventually became accustomed to the ghostly sounds. They began to wonder what had happened to these restless spirits to make them haunt the house. They decided to try to find out.

The Camerons discovered an underground graveyard on the grounds near the house. They also found a secret room in the basement where runaway slaves were once hidden in the days before the Civil War.

When Harold hired Enoch, a very old man who used to work at the mansion as a young boy, the missing facts were finally pieced together.

A terrible crime had occurred in 1864. The fifteen-year-old daughter of the family that lived in the house at that time was assaulted and murdered by Ben, the coachman. He lured her out of the house by telling her that she needed to come see her injured pony in the barn. The girl's body was found in the nearby creek, and Ben was executed for his crime. The heavy footsteps outside the house were those of Ben's ghost!

The lady of the house couldn't cope with the loss of her only child. She was pained by anything that reminded her of her daughter, so she cleaned the library because her daughter had loved that room.

One day the mother walked up to the top floor and hung herself from the front window. It was this woman's ghostly footsteps the family heard inside the house!

After two years, the Camerons moved out of the house on Plum Tree Lane. They never came back. The new owners decided to remodel the large mansion and turn it into an apartment house. They never had trouble filling the units—all except for one. The room that had been the library has always stayed empty!

Nothing But Trouble

It may be hard to believe, but ghosts don't always haunt dark and gloomy houses located near cemeteries or built over ancient Indian burial grounds. Nor do they always die by violence or suffer a great injustice that must be righted before their spirits can rest in peace.

Take, for example, a modern colonial house, built in 1966 and located in a small town in Massachusetts. Strange incidents have occurred at this rather normal-looking two-story home. But most people hesitate to call the place haunted. Listen to the story of the family who lives in the house. Then you be the judge!

"Let your cat in already. It's cold outside," said a friend of the family one winter evening. "Can't you hear it clawing at the screen door?"

"I hear it," the owner replied.

"So do something. I think it's crawling up the screen!"

"I can't do anything," said the owner, "because the cats are already inside the house, and we don't even have a screen door!"

"Then what's making that noise?" asked the friend, thoroughly perplexed.

"You tell me," replied the owner.

Several days later, the owner's daughter and grandson were sitting in the kitchen. The daughter heard a car drive into the garage, a motor turn off, and a car door slam. Then someone walked through the garage and up the cellar steps, opened the door, and walked through the den and into the kitchen. The daughter turned around to say hello and saw . . . no one! When she went to the garage, it was empty.

Even today, the family hears strange knockings in the house, mysterious footsteps, and creaking doors. Often the lights, water faucets, and appliances are turned on and off. Can ghosts turn on radios or washing machines?

The owner thinks the strange incidents began when several very old family portraits, dating back to the 1840s, were hung in the living room.

Is there some connection between the pictures and the ghostly happenings? It's possible, but can ghosts from the midnineteenth century drive cars or operate blenders?

The owner's family isn't afraid. If strange things happen, one would go outside and sit on the porch until other people come home. But they do feel a bit uneasy. After all, these things keep happening and there's no logical explanation for them.

Do ghosts really haunt this house, or is it the overactive imagination of the human inhabitants? Are there really troublesome spirits moving about, or just someone's forgetfulness in turning off lights and radios?

D. D. Home

It was December 1868, and the famous medium D. D. Home was giving a séance. Home was known for his power to communicate with the dead. As a physical medium, his typical séance included objects that moved, musical instruments that played by themselves, and other visible phenomena.

Those present at the séance were the Master of Lindsay, Viscount Adare, and Captain Charles Wynne. They were seated around the table as Home went into a trance.

"Do not be afraid," Home told the three men. "Do not leave your seats."

The medium then got up and walked into the next room, and the men heard a window open.

Within seconds, Home appeared, standing upright, *outside* the window of the room in which the three men sat. He then opened the window and glided in, feet first.

What is especially remarkable about this is that the windows were several stories off the ground! There was a very narrow ledge under the windows, but it was not wide enough to stand on. Therefore, Home must have *floated* through the air to get from one window to the next! All three witnesses testified that this was exactly what took place.

They shouldn't have been surprised, since Home was famous for spectacular phenomena. During a trance, he often levitated, rising up off the ground and floating to the ceiling with his arms above his head. Sometimes he even grew five or six inches taller during a séance while under spiritual control!

Home usually gave sittings in the bright light of day because he had nothing to hide. Participants often clearly saw strange moving lights, phantom hands that melted away, and tables that moved or rose in the air. Once Home placed his face into the burning coals of a fireplace without injury.

Throughout his career, Home was subjected to thorough investigation and testing. Many mediums at that time used trickery and fraud to deceive people. Never once was Home found to have "cheated" during a sitting!

During a séance, an investigator reported that "the table was seen to rise completely from the

floor and floated about in the air for several seconds." One man actually sat on top of the table,
and it still moved around!

Throughout Home's life, nonbelievers attempted to come up with explanations as to how
he accomplished such incredible feats at his séances. Some say he hypnotized participants into
believing these amazing things happened. Others
say the séance participants were Home's followers,
who would never doubt the ability of their leader
and might have imagined or exaggerated what actually took place. But no matter how hard they
tried, these nonbelievers could find no evidence of
trickery.

Were the spirits of the dead responsible for
Home's spectacular séances? There is no question
that he possessed amazing powers that have, so
far, been unequaled and remain unexplained.

Borley Rectory

What ghostly phenomena have *not* taken place at Borley Rectory? The answer is very few.

Since the 1860s, scores of people have reported mysterious and unexplained occurrences at Borley Rectory, near Sudbury in Suffolk, England. (A rectory is the house in which a minister lives.)

There have been sounds of whispering, horses galloping, church music, bells ringing, footsteps, knocking, bumps, thuds, wailing, rustling, crashing, and windows breaking.

People have seen the ghosts of a nun, a headless man, a figure in gray, a girl in white, a coach drawn by horses, and other shadowy figures. There have been wall writings, lighted windows, swinging blinds, cold spots, good and bad odors, and unexplained footprints.

It seems that Borley Rectory has been the center of supernatural disturbances for some time. To discover why, a look back at the history of the area is necessary.

Records show that a monastery existed in Borley as early as the thirteenth century. One story of that time that may be true is told of a monk from the monastery who fell in love with a local nun. The two planned to run away together, but they were caught and punished. The monk was hanged and, according to legend, a brick wall was built to seal the nun, alive, in the cellar.

In the years that followed, residents reported seeing the ghost of a nun near the monastery. But it wasn't until 1863, when the Reverend Henry Bull built a new rectory on the exact site, that incidents began to happen more frequently.

A nursemaid reported hearing ghostly footsteps. The Bull daughters saw the nun several times, and the cook saw a strange figure in the garden who suddenly disappeared.

Henry's son, the Reverend Harry Bull, and his family also saw the ghost of the nun. Their servants claimed to have seen a ghost coach with ghost horses.

The Cooper family, who lived in the cottage near the rectory, also saw the coach and horses, heard strange noises, and were terrified by a black shape in their bedroom.

After Harry Bull died in 1927, the Reverend Smith moved into the rectory with his family. He called in psychic Harry Price to investigate. When Price arrived at the rectory, he was met with showers of stones and other unusual activity. The Smith family couldn't cope with the ghosts and moved out, but Price remained to study the phenomena.

In 1930, Reverend Foyster and his family moved in, and more violent incidents were recorded. On several occasions, Foyster was pelted with stones, and his wife was thrown from her bed. Doors locked, music played, and bottles smashed, all seemingly on their own. After five difficult years, the Foysters, too, left the rectory.

In 1937, Harry Price rented it for a year. He recruited a random cross-section of people to act as impartial observers of the ghostly phenomena. Incidents were often witnessed by several people at a time and records were kept. Eventually Price gathered enough material to write two books about the Borley Rectory.

Several new stories emerged about the identity of the mysterious nun. One stated that Henry Waldegrave, whose family had owned the land long ago, married a French woman who was a former nun and later murdered her in the rectory. Another said the nun was Arabella Waldegrave, who was a spy against the British Commonwealth, and that she, too, was murdered at Borley.

A mysterious fire in 1939 burned the rectory to the ground. In 1943, Harry Price and several others dug through the ruins and found a jawbone of a woman and part of a human skull. Could this have been the remains of the unhappy nun whose ghost haunted the area? Price laid the bones to rest in a Christian burial.

The strange incidents continued at Borley even after the fire. Harry Price was still involved in studying the mysterious events when he died in 1949. Years after his death, some accused Price of staging many of the ghostly incidents. Yet strange happenings occurred and were reported by numerous people before *and* after Harry Price ever became involved.

Were the noises people heard just the scratchings of rats and birds in the rectory attic? Did mischievous village boys throw stones and bottles at the house, causing loud thuds and crashing sounds? Were the ghostly figures just hallucinations or real people who were mistakenly identified?

Or is the ground around Borley a haunted place of power that allows certain psychically gifted people to see the ghosts? For example, in one incident a man clearly saw the spirit of a woman in a long white gown, while his companion only heard the rustle of trees and bushes.

Photographers have noticed that after developing their photos of the churchyard at Borley, strange, unexplained shapes and faces appear in them. Yet they didn't see these images when they took the pictures!

Whatever the explanation, Borley Church and the site of the rectory still make many people very uneasy. Some people say it still looks and feels haunted, but most visitors don't stay long enough to find out!

The Divining Dowser

A bacon-curing plant in Waterford, Ireland, needed a large supply of water to process its bacon. The owners decided to dig a well on their property to tap into a natural water source below.

Several holes were dug by engineers, but none was successful in reaching water. One seven-inch hole, which was more than 1,000 feet deep, yielded no water at all!

The manager finally sent for a water diviner named John Mullins, who practiced the ancient art of dowsing. Mullins used a forked stick made of hazelwood about twelve or fifteen inches long. He held each end between his second and third fingers. He then walked around the property, holding the stick horizontally in front of him. Almost immediately, the stick bent slightly by itself.

"Mark that spot," instructed Mullins to the plant manager.

As Mullins moved on, several other places were marked. A few clerks from the plant watched Mullins carefully. Some even held on to the stick, placing their hands over his. "The stick is moving by itself," said the clerks in amazement. "His hands are completely still!" At one spot in particular, the stick lifted itself up and twisted around until it broke!

"There's water here," Mullins declared. "It's not more than eighty feet down. Try this place first."

A hole was dug. At about 75 feet, water was discovered. When the well was completed, it pumped about 2,000 gallons per hour, much to the delight of the plant owners.

How could Mullins have located the exact spot at which the water supply could be obtained? How did he correctly predict the depth of the water? And finally, how did the dowser succeed where engineers and geologists failed?

Dowsing may have existed as early as prehistoric man. The practice is still widespread and very successful today. The big question is, how and why does it work?

Some believe a force, such as vibrations, electromagnetic waves, or even radiation is emitted from the water. This force then affects the stick or even,

perhaps, the mind of the dowser. Others say that dowsing is a psychic experience. The dowser's muscles respond to extrasensory stimulation, causing the stick to move. Many dowsers feel strange or even sick when the rod moves in their hands. Some have described it as "a tingling or electric shock," "a trembling," or "a spasm."

Dowsers have been successful in finding hidden or missing objects as well as underground water. Some even use metal rods instead of a forked dowsing stick. Others use nothing at all. They just seem to know where the water or object is located.

No one knows exactly how or why dowsing is successful. What's important is that it seems to work!

Rajah

"I may not be back this afternoon," eighteen-year-old Ruth Rockwell announced to her sister-in-law. Ruth was a moody girl and very much obsessed with death. She believed in reincarnation. She felt that after people died they were reborn into a new body or new form of life.

"Good-bye, Rajah," said Ruth to the large and gentle Great Dane who stood quietly as he watched her leave. She patted his head and walked out the door.

"What a strange young woman!" thought Mrs. Rockwell as she went about her morning chores. It was November 11, 1930. Ruth had been staying with them for several months.

The Rockwells lived on a small farm in New

York's Westchester County. Donald, Ruth's brother, took the train each morning to his job in Manhattan.

At three o'clock that afternoon, Mrs. Rockwell was sitting in the living room when Rajah suddenly ran upstairs. He came back down with a pillow in his mouth and placed it at the astonished woman's feet.

"How thoughtful, Rajah! A cushion for my feet!" she exclaimed with a chuckle. "What are you up to?"

Rajah raced back upstairs and returned carrying a coat in his mouth. He laid it on top of the pillow.

"Why, that's Ruth's coat," said Mrs. Rockwell.

Again, the dog ran back upstairs and this time came down with one of Ruth's hats.

The Great Dane then lay down, put his head on the pillow, hat, and coat, and began whining and whimpering.

"Poor boy," said Mrs. Rockwell. "What are you upset about? Did Ruth forget her hat and coat? And is that her pillow, too?"

Sure enough, Rajah had taken the pillow from Ruth's bed. After a few minutes, Mrs. Rockwell returned the items to their proper places. She was still thinking about the dog's odd behavior when the phone rang a half-hour later. It was the police.

"Mrs. Rockwell," the officer said. "I'm sorry to have to inform you that your sister-in-law, Ruth Rockwell, is dead."

Mrs. Rockwell was shocked. The officer related that Ruth had been a passenger on a small private plane that flew people on short sightseeing trips over Long Island. The pilot recalled that she had been very nervous on the flight and seemed to be praying.

"But a lot of people are nervous if it's their first plane ride," the pilot declared. "I felt the airplane sway a bit, and when I looked around she was gone. It was as if she had disappeared into thin air. It's an awful tragedy."

Ruth had jumped out of the plane and was killed. It was the first time a woman had ever committed suicide in such a way.

When the Rockwells returned home that night from the police station, weary and numb with grief, Mrs. Rockwell told her husband about Rajah's strange behavior.

"What time did you say this happened?" he asked.

"About three o'clock," replied his wife.

"That's almost the exact time Ruth was killed," he declared. "It's almost as if Rajah knew what had happened."

Suddenly the Great Dane, who had been lying next to their bed, jumped up, ran to the window, and started barking furiously. Then he rushed back, put his paws on Mrs. Rockwell's knees, and growled in the direction of the street. Again Rajah ran to the window, snarling and baring his teeth.

The hair on his neck and back stood up as he barked and growled.

Mr. Rockwell looked out the window. "No one's out there, boy," he said, trying to calm the usually gentle dog.

"You mean, no one you can see!" said his wife nervously. It was nine o'clock.

Later the Rockwells discovered a note written by Ruth before her suicide. It said, "If there is a spirit world, I will attempt to communicate with someone in the family at nine o'clock."

Did Rajah see the ghost of Ruth? Can dogs instinctively know things that people don't? Do they have an extra sense that allows them to see what humans are unable to?

After a time, things returned to normal in the Rockwell home. The Great Dane often sat next to Ruth's favorite chair, resting his head on its arm as if he was waiting to be stroked by someone who wasn't there.

Ghost Toys

"Can you help me, please?" the woman customer asked the salesclerk at a Toys " " Us store
in Sunnyvale, California. "This talking doll must
be defective. It hasn't said a word, and my daughter is very disappointed."

"Let me try it, ma'am," said the clerk. She tilted
the doll, pressed its stomach, and turned it upside
down. The toy was stubbornly silent.

"Why don't you pick out another one and I'll
send this one back to the manufacturer," she said,
putting the doll into its box.

"Thank you, dear," smiled the woman. She
turned and walked away down the nearest aisle.

"Another satisfied customer," thought the salesclerk to herself. She closed the lid of the box and

was about to shelve it when she suddenly heard sounds. The clerk put her ear to the box.

"Mama, Mama, Mama," the doll repeated over and over again. After a period of silence, the doll talked again. Puzzled, the clerk took the toy to the stockroom. There, the doll actually started to make crying sounds!

"Very strange," thought the clerk later as she sat alone in the employee lounge. "The voice mechanism must be jammed or something."

Suddenly the bulletin board on the wall started to move back and forth.

"Anybody here?" said the clerk nervously. She looked around and found she was still alone.

As she stared at the bulletin board, a stack of papers piled on top of the nearby refrigerator floated slowly to the floor, one sheet at a time.

"Okay, that's it. Let me out of here!" she declared out loud. The frightened clerk had to stop herself from breaking into a run as she left the lounge.

Other employees at this Toys " " Us have experienced unexplained and mysterious incidents. One manager had just locked up the store for the night when he heard a loud banging inside the building. Could someone have been locked inside accidentally? He went back in, but the building was empty. Shrugging his shoulders, the manager locked the doors once more. As he walked to his car, the loud banging started up again. This happened several more times before the man simply ignored the banging and went home.

Another clerk heard her name called over and over again by a mysterious voice and felt invisible fingers in her hair. One customer complained that the water faucets in the ladies' room were turning on and off by themselves. Merchandise moved during the night, shelves fell over, and lights turned on and off without explanation.

As the incidents continued, more and more employees began to believe the store was haunted. Several investigated the history of the area in which the store was built, hoping to find clues to identify the ghost or ghosts.

At first some workers believed the ghost of Martin Murphy, the founder of Sunnyvale, haunted the toy store. But after psychic Sylvia Brown spent a night in the store, most believed the restless spirit was that of a preacher named Yon Johnson.

Yon had lived with a family whose farm was on the site of the toy store at the turn of the century. He loved a girl named Elizabeth, who may have been the daughter of Martin Murphy. She eventually married someone else, but Yon never stopped loving her and remained a bachelor all his life.

Sylvia Brown had visions of Yon walking through the store, which he still saw as the farm on which he lived. She saw him pumping water from a spring, which employees later discovered had once been located right under the toy store.

Do the mysterious happenings in Sunnyvale have logical but overlooked explanations? Is the ghost of restless and lovesick Yon still searching for his lost love? Or do the employees of the toy store have overactive imaginations?

Perhaps we will never know the answer. But now, whenever something strange and unexplained happens at this particular toy store, the employees just say, "Yonny's at it again!"

Fire!

The dinner party had just begun in Göteborg, Sweden. The famous scientist and psychic Emanuel Swedenborg was among sixteen guests on the evening of July 19, 1759.

Swedenborg had studied engineering and written books about the animal kingdom, the human brain, and psychology. Since 1747, however, he had devoted himself only to matters of a spiritual nature, such as psychic visions and communication with the spirit world.

Suddenly, just after dinner had been served, Swedenborg stood up and walked quickly out of the house without speaking to anyone.

When the host of the party came into the room, he noticed that Swedenborg was missing. "Where did the doctor go? He was here only a minute ago," the host asked one of the guests.

"He stepped outside," replied the woman. "But he had the strangest expression on his face."

Swedenborg soon returned. "Here he is now! Emanuel, come sit down. You look ill and you're trembling," the host exclaimed.

"Whatever is wrong?" asked the concerned woman.

Swedenborg began to speak slowly. "I see a fire, a horrible blaze in Stockholm. It's out of control, racing through the city."

"But that's three hundred miles from here!" whispered the woman, somewhat astonished.

For several hours, Swedenborg described the details of the fire as it was occurring. "It has already destroyed my friend's home, and now it's threatening my own house," he said sadly.

The guests were startled, but the party continued. Finally, at approximately 8 P.M., Swedenborg made an announcement. "The fire is out. It has been stopped just three doors from my home!"

The next day, everyone wondered if there really had been a fire. Was Swedenborg's vision accurate? Was it all a trick? There was no telegraph or radio at that time, so it was impossible to find out the truth immediately.

Two days after the dinner party, a courier arrived from Stockholm with news. He confirmed that there had been a devastating fire in the Swedish city. As details of the disaster emerged, they matched everything Swedenborg had described. Most amazing was the fact that the blaze had indeed been halted only three houses from Swedenborg's residence, just as he had stated!

This incident of clairvoyance (which means to become aware of events or objects without the use of the usual five senses) was verified by numerous witnesses at the dinner party. Although the case was widely investigated, no reason or explanation for Swedenborg's vision could be given, other than extrasensory perception.

Was it a clear case of clairvoyance? If not, how could Swedenborg have known so many details about a fire that happened three hundred miles away?

Edgar Cayce

In 1904, Edgar Cayce (pronounced *KAY*-cee), a salesman in a bookstore in Bowling Green, Kentucky, lay down on an operating table at the local doctor's office. He crossed his hands over his stomach, shut his eyes, and breathed deeply a few times.

Observing Cayce in the room were several well-known doctors from Bowling Green, along with a college professor. Within minutes, Cayce was in a deep sleep and his eyelids began to flicker. One of the physicians walked over to the table.

"Mr. Cayce," he said, "I'm presently treating a six-year-old boy named Jonathan Brooks. You don't know him. He lives on South Main Street in Bowling Green and is sick in bed right now. Will you please describe his physical condition for me?"

After a few seconds, Cayce, still sleeping in a trancelike state, replied, "Yes, we have the body. There's excessive fluid in the right lung, and no air can be inhaled into the lung. The left lung was once involved but is almost normal now. There's also an inflammation in the stomach."

"Thank you, Mr. Cayce," said the doctor. Turning to the others in the room, the physician declared, "Gentlemen, Mr. Cayce's diagnosis is perfectly correct! We will continue this demonstration with additional test cases, all of whom are total strangers to Mr. Cayce."

The sleeping man went on to diagnose other patients correctly and, in some cases, prescribed particular medicine or treatment. While in his trance, he was able to pinpoint abnormalities and diseases. Then he would suggest a remedy without ever seeing or examining the actual patient!

This extraordinary man, with no background or training in medicine or surgery, gave thousands of medically correct "readings" throughout his life, many over long distances.

He was called a healer, a clairvoyant, a seer, and a psychic, sensitive to supernatural and extrasensory forces. But Edgar Cayce, a deeply religious man, believed he simply had a gift from God.

Born on March 18, 1877, Cayce was a farm boy who showed an early interest in religion and the Bible. At age fifteen, he was hit on the head by a baseball and went into a coma. During the coma, he spoke clearly to his parents, prescribing what they should do to make him well. This was his first reading.

During another illness when he was twenty-three, Cayce lost his voice for ten months. When all medical help failed, a hypnotist named Al C. Layne put him into a trance in a last-ditch effort to cure him. Under hypnosis, Cayce began talking normally in a full, steady voice. He explained that there was a partial paralysis of the vocal cords and then prescribed his own cure. The hypnotist realized the potential of Cayce's power. The readings continued and Cayce's reputation grew.

Cayce cured his wife's tuberculosis and his son's partial blindness. He gave correct medical readings for patients hundreds of miles away. All he needed were their names and exact locations.

He used his power in other areas, too. He sometimes helped the police solve difficult crimes. In one case, Cayce gave the exact location of a murder weapon. The police wanted to arrest him as the murderer because they were convinced that only the criminal would know such details!

Later in his life, Cayce gave "life readings" in which he told people about their past lives (reincarnation). Cayce himself believed he had been, in previous lives, an Egyptian high priest named Ra Ta, an English soldier in colonial times named John Bainbridge, and a Persian warrior named Uhjltd. He claimed he had also been a Greek named Xenon and a follower of Jesus named Lucius.

Edgar Cayce died on January 3, 1945. At the time of his death, he was receiving four to five hundred letters daily asking for help. To fulfill this demand, Cayce pushed himself to give eight readings a day.

He was called the "most gifted psychic of our time." Cayce once said about his powers, "I don't do anything you can't do."

Disaster at Sea

It was a cold April evening. The mid-Atlantic Ocean was covered in thick fog as a giant ocean liner sped along. The huge ship was traveling at more than twenty knots—too fast for such poor weather conditions. Almost 800 feet long, the ship carried only twenty-four lifeboats, certainly not enough for the 3,000 passengers aboard.

Dead ahead and partially obscured by the fog lay a giant iceberg. Most of the large mass of ice was hidden below the surface of the water. Unaware of the danger, the crew of the luxury liner continued on a collision course with the iceberg.

Does this scene sound familiar? Could this be a description of the *Titanic* disaster of April 14, 1912? Guess again! It is a description of the fictional ship *Titan* from a novel called *Futility* by Morgan Robertson. The amazing thing is that this novel was written in 1898, fourteen years *before* the *Titanic*'s first and final voyage!

There are many similarities between the fictitious novel and the actual event. To begin with, the names of the two ships are nearly identical. Both were described as the largest and fastest vessels afloat—"unsinkable" and "indestructible." Each ship had three propellers and two masts, and carried the same number of passengers.

Did the author of *Futility* have a prophetic vision of what was to happen years in the future? Or was the similarity of his fictional account just a coincidence?

Warnings of impending disaster aboard luxury liners occurred as early as the 1880s. A journalist named W. T. Stead warned that ships didn't carry enough lifeboats for their crews and passengers. In 1892, Stead wrote a fictional account of an ocean liner's colliding with an iceberg in the Atlantic. In the story, many died in the icy waters after the ship sank.

This same journalist was aboard the *Titanic* on April 10, 1912, when it sailed from Southampton, England. Stead was among the more than fifteen hundred victims who died in the freezing waters of the Atlantic when the great liner went down. Ironically, despite his warnings about the lack of lifeboats, he became a victim himself.

Many people had premonitions about the *Titanic* disaster. An engineer turned down a job in the *Titanic*'s engine room because he felt something terrible would happen. Others felt superstitious about sailing on the maiden voyage of any ship. The wealthy banker J. Pierpont Morgan was one of those who canceled his sailing plans for this reason. A man had a dream that the *Titanic* was shipwrecked, so he booked passage on another ship. One woman, watching the giant liner steam out to sea, screamed to her husband, "It's going to sink! Do something! Save them!"

On April 14, four days after the *Titanic* set out to sea, the ocean was covered in fog. The ship sped along at 22½ knots. There had been warnings of icebergs, but the crew was not worried. After all, the *Titanic* was "unsinkable"!

At 11:40 P.M., the luxury ship hit the iceberg below the waterline, tearing open its hull. Most passengers felt only a small shudder. Five compartments flooded immediately and the rest filled gradually. Seawater poured in and the ship slowly began sinking.

Over two thousand people were aboard, but there were only twenty lifeboats. About 700 survived, even though many of the lifeboats weren't even close to being filled to capacity before they were lowered into the water.

Hundreds froze or drowned in the water, screaming for help that never came. A large num-

ber stayed on board as the *Titanic* rose straight up out of the water, then sank quickly and quietly to the depths of the ocean.

Why were there so many premonitions and warnings of the *Titanic* disaster? Were they true cases of precognition, clairvoyance relating to the future?

Huge icebergs, bad weather, speedy ocean liners, and the lack of lifeboats were a dangerous combination. Was a horrible accident bound to happen eventually?

Some good did come out of this disaster. The sinking of the *Titanic* resulted in the passage of many new safety rules and regulations for ocean-going ships. With this knowledge and awareness, many such disasters at sea were avoided in the future.

The Haunted Family

It was 1973 when the Smurl family moved into the house in West Pittston, Pennsylvania. Soon afterward, their troubles began.

Small things happened at first. An unexplained grease stain on the carpet kept coming back even after repeated cleanings. One night, the TV set burst into flames. Mysterious scratches appeared on the sink and tub after the bathroom was remodeled. The toilet flushed by itself. The radio played when it wasn't even plugged in. Drawers opened and closed in the bedrooms.

Then, more frightening things began to happen.

"Janet," whispered the soft, strange voice. Janet Smurl was alone in the basement doing laundry. At least she thought she was alone.

"Janet," whispered the voice again.

She whirled around but saw no one. Thoroughly shaken, she backed up the stairs slowly and slammed the door to the basement. Had she imagined a voice calling to her?

Several days passed. Janet was in the kitchen ironing. She looked up and saw a black form floating toward her. As it moved closer, she smelled a strange odor and felt a cold chill. The shape glided into the living room and vanished.

One evening, something grabbed Janet's leg and tried to pull her off the bed. Her husband, Jack, had to tug with all his strength to keep her from being pulled away.

At night the family regularly heard banging and pounding inside the walls of the house. The family dog was picked up by an unseen force and thrown against the kitchen door. One of the Smurl's four daughters was struck by a heavy overhead light that had somehow torn itself out of the ceiling.

The Smurls, who were Roman Catholic, asked two priests to bless their house. For several days after each blessing, the house was quiet. But each time the trouble started up again.

Demonologists Ed and Lorraine Warren were invited to visit. Using Lorraine's powers as a medium, they determined that three spirits and a demon haunted the house.

One spirit was an elderly woman who was found to be confused and harmless. A younger female spirit turned out to be insane and violent. The third spirit was a man who seemed to be controlled by the demon, who Lorraine said was "here to create chaos and destroy the family!"

According to Ed Warren, the demon and spirits had always been in the house but had been quiet until now. They became active by drawing on the energy of the Smurls' teenage daughters.

Armed with holy water blessed by the church, the Smurls continued to resist the demon, who in turn became more violent. Jack was physically attacked and bitten in the shower. The rapping and scratching noises continued inside the walls. Terrible odors and drastic drops in temperature occurred without warning.

The Warrens brought in Father Robert McKenna of Connecticut who performed two separate exorcisms. An exorcism is a church ritual to cast out demons. Both were unsuccessful, and the haunting continued.

The Smurls' sixteen-year-old daughter was attacked in the shower. A younger daughter was mysteriously lifted off her bed and suspended in midair. Jack was thrown to the floor. Another daughter was picked up and hurled out of bed during the night. The noises went on and on.

When Jack and Janet spent a weekend away from their home, the demon followed them to their motel and continued to attack them. Later, when

the family went on a camping trip, the demon again followed them.

Would they ever be free?

There were additional attacks on the family, even more vicious and brutal than before. The Smurls retaliated by sprinkling holy water and saying prayers.

In the hope that they could get more help, the family went public, describing their problems on television and in newspapers and magazines. Scores of curious people drove by their home and camped-out on their lawn. Neighbors and friends were very supportive. The Smurls found out that six other homes on their block were experiencing rapping noises, bad odors, and screaming sounds.

A prayer meeting was organized. Fifty women and twenty men filled the Smurl home, each of them holding a candle as they all prayed together.

Jack and Janet had hoped to have several priests participate in a mass exorcism at the house, but the diocese of the Catholic Church declined to participate. Priests were sent to stay overnight at the Smurl house, but they heard and saw nothing unusual. Therefore, the church felt there was no proof of a haunting.

Father McKenna returned and performed a third exorcism. This time, friends and relatives held daily prayer vigils during and after the ritual. Within days, the scent of roses filled the Smurl home!

Weeks went by without incident. Months passed, and the Smurls enjoyed the peace and quiet of a normal family. But it didn't last.

In December 1986, the haunting began again. The following year, the Smurl family moved to another town in Pennsylvania.

Will the demon follow them there? Will they ever be really free again? Only time will tell. In the meantime, their continued faith and love for one another helps the family to cope with whatever each new day brings.

The Tower of London

The night guard at the Tower of London stood frozen and paralyzed with fear. This can't be happening, he thought to himself. I must be dreaming!

There, in plain sight of the guard, was a woman dressed in sixteenth-century clothing, accompanied by a group of men and women in similar dress. They walked the grounds of the Tower Green.

As the guard watched in horror, he realized that something was very wrong. He studied the faces of the strange procession, and then he suddenly understood, just before he fainted, what was so peculiar about the first woman.

"She has no head!" he exclaimed, and then he blacked out.

When you are a guard on the night shift at the

Tower of London, seeing ghosts is not that uncommon. The tower has been called one of the world's bloodiest historic sites! Used mainly as a prison and place of execution, hundreds of people were hanged and beheaded in the tower. Kings, queens, counts, and countesses were among those who met their deaths within the tower walls. Their ghosts reportedly still haunt the grounds.

Many towers, buildings, and yards make up the eighteen acres known as the Tower of London. Today, it is a popular tourist attraction where the crown jewels are kept.

The headless noblewoman the guard saw was very likely the ghost of Anne Boleyn, the second wife of King Henry VIII. She has been said to appear with or without her head, leading a group of lords and ladies of the court. Anne was beheaded on the Tower Green in 1536 because she couldn't bear King Henry a son. But Anne had the last laugh on Henry. Her daughter, Elizabeth I, became Queen of England and reigned for forty-five years!

In those days, most executions were performed with an ax to the neck. Sometimes several blows were needed to cut off the unfortunate victim's head. Anne was afraid of the ax and had a swordsman from France brought in to behead her in a single stroke.

Over the years, other tower guards have reported seeing ghosts. One terrified sentry saw a

stretcher carried by two men. On the stretcher was a body with its head tucked under one arm.

The ghosts of the twelve-year-old boy-king, Edward V, and his younger brother, Richard, are reported to have appeared in the Bloody Tower. They were imprisoned in the tower in the late fifteenth century and may have been murdered there.

Another tower ghost is the seventy-year-old Countess of Salisbury, who was ordered beheaded by Henry VIII in 1541. She refused to bend over the chopping block, and the executioner chased her around the Tower Green with his ax!

The ghost of Lady Jane Grey was seen by two tower guards in 1957 on the roof of the Salt Tower. First, Lady Jane watched as her husband was executed. Then she herself was beheaded at the age of fifteen.

If ghosts are the spirits of restless and unhappy people, the Tower of London, with its bloody history, has reason to have countless numbers of them roaming around.

The Gray Ghost

"No sign of the gray ghost," said the director quietly to the producer of a lavish American musical. The two men were rehearsing the show at the Theatre Royal in London, England.

"Did I hear you say 'ghost'?" asked the young actress who had a supporting role in the show.

The director took the young woman aside. "You may not believe this, but the theater is haunted," he said.

The young woman's eyes widened.

"Before you begin to think I'm crazy," explained the director, "let me assure you that the gray ghost—some call him the gray man—has been seen by hundreds of people for more than a hundred years."

"I didn't know this place was that old," declared the young woman.

"This building was built in 1812," the director continued. "Three previous buildings on this site were either destroyed by fire or torn down."

The famous Theatre Royal has been the site of many hit musicals such as *Hello Dolly!*, *Oklahoma*, and *South Pacific*. The ghost that haunts this theater is unlike other spirits, however. He doesn't intentionally scare or terrorize anyone, nor does he make any sounds. He simply walks around the theater.

"People say he comes out of the wall on the upper circle level, where we are now, and walks to the other side of the theater," the director continued. "The ghost only appears in the daytime, and sometimes when there's a matinee. In fact, some members of the audience have actually seen him during a performance," he added.

"Who was he and why is he haunting the theater?" asked the young actress.

"No one really knows," the director answered. "But in 1848, a tiny room was discovered bricked-up inside the walls of the theater. Inside the room was a skeleton with a dagger in its ribs."

"That explains it!" she exclaimed. "Maybe the gray ghost is the unhappy spirit of the man who was murdered so many years ago. The murderer obviously hid the body."

"The bones were given a proper burial in a cemetery, but the ghost keeps appearing in the theater," added the director.

"I don't want to sound offensive or anything," said the actress, "but why are you so interested in this ghost? It sounds as if you're actually waiting for him to appear."

"This may sound strange to you, but if the ghost is seen before a new show starts, it's considered good luck," the director explained. "In the past, the gray ghost has appeared before hit shows, but he was nowhere to be seen at all the flops."

The young actress nodded. "Now I understand. You want him to come before the curtain goes up tonight, so the musical will be a hit!"

"Let me put it this way," the director said, smiling. "The show is great. The tunes are great. The cast is great. I'm convinced it will be a hit. But it would be nice if the gray ghost put in an appearance—as insurance, of course."

"So what does he look like?" the woman questioned.

"He wears a long, dark gray cape over a coat with ruffled sleeves," the director explained. "He carries a sword and wears riding boots."

The actress's eyes grew wide again. "Does he wear a big, dark hat over a powdered gray wig?"

"Why, yes, but how did you know?" the director asked, puzzled. Then, following her gaze, he turned slowly and looked behind him.

The director and actress stared openmouthed at

the sight of the gray ghost across the room, some thirty-five feet away. Obviously a gentleman, he moved silently across the room, keeping his distance. Then he passed through the door and out of sight.

The man and woman slowly turned to look at each other. "You'd better close your mouth before a fly settles in it. We have just seen the gray ghost!" the director said, grinning from ear to ear. "Sweetheart, we have a hit!"

He reached over, gave the actress a bear hug, and ran off. "I've got to tell the producer!"

The young actress sat down and took a deep breath. "Tonight is opening night and I have just seen a ghost! Oh, well," she shrugged. "That's show business."

The Bell Witch

At first there were unusual noises at the Bell House in Robertson County, Tennessee—knocking, scraping, clawing, and flapping sounds. Then it got much worse for John Bell, his wife, Lucy, and their nine children.

The year was 1817. A mischievous ghost, called a poltergeist, began to pull sheets and blankets off the beds and make gulping, choking, and strangling sounds. Then it began to throw stones and turn chairs upside down. The disturbances seemed to focus around twelve-year-old Betsy Bell.

One night the poltergeist yanked the hair of two of the children so hard that they began to scream in pain. Betsy was scratched and slapped across the face by an unseen hand. Sometimes visitors to the house even received slaps!

The poltergeist began making whistling sounds, which gradually developed into a low gasping. Some believe that Betsy unknowingly provided the energy for the disturbances.

The voice identified itself as a witch named Old Kate Batts. It had several other personalities, including an Indian and a man.

"I am a spirit who was once very happy," declared the witch, "but I have been disturbed and now am unhappy."

The witch eventually turned her focus to John Bell, declaring she would torment and kill him! Soon afterward, Bell's tongue swelled and he couldn't eat for days at a time. The witch cursed at him and used bad language.

The spirit yanked off the man's shoes. She hit him in the face so hard he went into convulsions. The witch shrieked with laughter at his agony. After three years of this abuse, Bell became physically ill and depressed.

The witch was still cruel to young Betsy, but she could also be nice. On Betsy's birthday, a basket of oranges and bananas appeared out of thin air as a gift to the girl.

John Bell took to his bed in 1820. His son found a nearly empty bottle of strange-looking medicine. The son heard the witch cackle, "I've got him this time."

When the doctor arrived at the house, he tested the unknown medicine by giving some to the cat, who died immediately. The next day, John Bell was also dead!

The witch then declared to the family, "I am going and will be gone for seven years." After that, all was calm in the Bell household.

Seven years later the noises began again. By this time, Betsy and most of the other children had already married and moved away. The noises were ignored by the rest of the family and ended after two weeks.

The strange story of the Bell witch was discussed in detail in a book written by John Bell's son Richard in 1846. What makes this case unusual is that most recorded poltergeists do not harm their victims. They may be annoying and playful, throwing dishes and moving furniture around, but they normally stop short of physical attack.

Did the witch, who seemed to get most of her energy from Betsy, torment and then kill John Bell because the young girl resented her father? If so, then why did the witch also torment Betsy? And how could she have returned to the Bell home seven years later if Betsy had already moved away?

One expert believes a house with nine children, many of them teenagers, provided plenty of energy for a particularly cruel and malicious poltergeist. The children were unhappy and disliked their very strict and disciplinary father.

The case of the Bell witch stands out as an exception among poltergeist incidents—one that will hopefully never be repeated.

Redsy

Ever since Redsy was a puppy, she would go with her master everywhere. The Irish setter especially loved to go on fishing trips. She enjoyed riding in her master's boat off the New England coast and was never bothered by the occasional choppiness and rough seas of the Atlantic Ocean.

On one particular day, her master, William Montgomery, had just finished stocking his boat. He was looking forward to a great day of flounder fishing. The weather couldn't have been more perfect; there wasn't a single cloud in the beautiful blue sky.

"Let's shove off, Redsy," said Montgomery. "Those fish are waiting for us."

Usually the dog needed little encouragement to

jump into the boat, but today was different. Redsy refused to move. She sat on shore and stared at her master.

"What's wrong with you, girl?" asked Montgomery. "Get in the boat!"

Redsy stood up and barked, but she refused to move off the dock.

"Come, Redsy," Montgomery commanded. "I said, into the boat."

But the more he insisted, the louder Redsy barked. It was obvious that the dog did not want anything to do with this particular fishing trip.

"I can't figure you out, Redsy. You always love to go fishing," declared Montgomery. "What's bothering you, girl?"

The man scratched his head and thought for a while. He stared out to sea and saw dozens of other fishermen heading toward the flounder banks in their boats.

For an instant, Montgomery considered going out alone and leaving the dog behind on the dock. But never in his memory could he recall Redsy acting so strangely. He remembered some of his friends saying that his dog had more sense than most people they knew. Montgomery figured that something wasn't right.

Maybe Redsy knows something I don't, he thought to himself. "Okay, girl, you win!" he said out loud. "The trip's off. Let's go home! It wouldn't have been fun without you anyway."

The dog jumped up and ran around excitedly in circles, relieved at the news.

An hour later, the beautiful blue sky was full of storm clouds. Without warning, galelike winds blew in from the sea. Enormous waves battered the New England coast, destroying beach cottages and smashing small boats. Some waves were almost forty feet high!

Of the fifty boats that set out that day to fish for flounder, few made it back to shore. More than six hundred people were killed. Years later, they called it the great hurricane of 1938!

That evening, William Montgomery gave Redsy an extra-special dinner. He even let her sit on his favorite chair. He didn't know how or why, but the dog had sensed the impending danger of the storm. Redsy had known that if they had set out to sea, they would probably never come back.

Was it extrasensory perception? Can a dog have a premonition or vision of danger? Was it animal instinct?

Whatever it was, William Montgomery knew full well that Redsy had saved his life. And for that, he was always grateful.

Ghost of a Young Man

Kathy was washing dishes in the kitchen of her new one-story home. Suddenly a shadow crossed the window. She glanced up from the sink and saw a young man walking by.

"Hello, can I help you?" she called to the stranger, who was rather shabbily dressed. He was heading toward the rear of her house.

Drying her hands, Kathy hurried to the back door to intercept him. Looking out, she saw the man walk slowly through the backyard garden and toward the large hedge that marked the end of the property. Then he disappeared! Kathy looked around, but there was no sign of the stranger!

Over the next month, she saw him many times, always dressed in the same shabby clothes. He walked in the same direction into the garden, his head down. Sometimes he passed through the hedge into the field beyond before he disappeared. Other times he vanished in the garden or near the kitchen window.

Kathy was sure she was seeing a ghost and finally told her husband, Bob. He chuckled after hearing her story.

I can tell he doesn't believe me, thought Kathy. Maybe he thinks I'm imagining it all. I even wonder that myself.

The man appeared to Kathy two or three times a week, but sometimes he showed up several times a day. In one twenty-four-hour period, she saw him walk the same route at least seven times!

One weekend, Kathy's mother was visiting Kathy and Bob. "Where's that young man I saw walking to the back of the house?" her mother asked.

"What young man?" replied Bob. "There's no one here."

When her mother described the stranger, it matched the description of the ghost Kathy had been seeing for weeks.

At least I'm not going out of my mind, Kathy thought. Someone else has seen him, too!

Bob finally believed Kathy. But soon afterward, just as suddenly as the ghostly man appeared, he disappeared for many months. So much time passed that Kathy and Bob forgot all about the strange intruder.

Then one morning, almost a year later, he appeared again.

"He came last October," Kathy declared, "and now he's here again this October!"

"We've got to get to the bottom of this," said Bob.

He went to the Institute of Psychical Research for help. After an investigation, researchers discovered that the house had once been part of a larger farm. There had been a path that ran near the house, through the garden and hedge, and into the field. A pond had been located in the middle of the field.

The owners of the farm had a son who attended the local university. The young man became very depressed and kept to himself. His parents didn't know how to help him feel better. The young man would often take long walks alone along the path, with his head down. He always seemed to be deep in thought as he walked.

One day in October, the farmer's son took his customary walk. But this time, when he got to the pond, he jumped in and drowned.

Every October, the ghost of the young man returns to retrace the final footsteps of his life. Over and over again, he walks until the month ends, and then he returns the following year.

Although Kathy and Bob understood the sad reason for this haunting, they never really felt comfortable with it. Eventually, they sold their home and moved away.

The Drums of Death

"This is a wonderful dinner, Lady Airlie," said the woman visitor to her gracious hostess as they enjoyed a lavish meal. "Thank you so much for inviting me to be your guest at Cortachy Castle."

"The pleasure is ours, madame," replied the smiling hostess.

The visitor paused, then said, "A strange thing occurred as I was dressing for dinner a short time ago."

"Do tell us, dear," said an interested Lord Airlie.

"Well," the woman began, "I heard music outside my window. Actually, it was the sound of a drummer playing near the castle."

Suddenly, all activity ceased at the dinner table.

The other guests cleared their throats and acted embarrassed. Lord Airlie turned as white as a ghost, and his wife looked very upset.

Oh dear, what have I said? thought the woman to herself. She decided to quickly change the subject. "The weather is quite lovely at this time of year in Scotland, don't you think? In London, it's still so damp and cold." Eventually the conversation started up again and things appeared to return to normal.

Later that evening, the woman was determined to find out what had made everyone so distressed at her mention of the drumming. Another guest explained to her that the castle was haunted by the ghost of a drummer boy. Many years ago, the boy angered a former lord. As punishment, the boy was forcibly pushed into his drum and thrown out of the castle tower to his death. Before he was killed, the boy had threatened to haunt the family forever. Since then the drum was reportedly heard before the deaths of several different family members.

"In fact, the drum was heard before the late Countess of Airlie died unexpectedly in her sleep several years ago," explained the guest.

The next day, the woman again heard the sounds of the drummer. She decided to leave the castle and visit friends in nearby Dundee. Apologizing to Lord and Lady Airlie, the woman was relieved to leave. She never wanted to hear those drums again!

Within hours, Lady Airlie was dead. She had left a note explaining that she knew the drum was sounding for her. Five years later, the drums were heard again when Lord Airlie was on a hunt. The following day, he was dead.

Thirty years passed. The music of the drums was heard again at Cortachy Castle. The current Lord Airlie was in the United States at the time and was not even aware that the drums were sounding. An hour later, he was dead.

Does the ghostly music of the drums foretell a death in the family? Are the people so terrified of the drums that they actually die of fright because they believe their time on Earth is up?

The twelfth Earl of Airlie died in 1968. His widow claims the drums were not heard by anyone prior to his death. Is the curse of the ghostly drummer boy finally over? Or was it all just a series of bizarre coincidences? Only time will tell.

The Lady in White

"Oh, no!" screamed Alex as he slammed his foot down hard on the brake. He had been driving along eastbound highway A677 on the way to Blackburn, in Lancashire, England, when a woman had run out of nowhere right in front of his car. He felt a sickening thud as the automobile hit the woman's body and then ran over her.

"My God, what did we hit?" exclaimed Alex's wife, who wasn't paying attention when the woman ran into the road.

As the car screeched to a stop, Alex couldn't keep himself from shaking.

"I think I've killed someone," he said, his voice thick with emotion. "I've got to find out if she's still alive."

Alex hurriedly got out of the car. He looked underneath and then behind the car, but there was no sign of a body. He searched up and down the road and off the shoulder on both sides but found nothing.

He returned to the car, shaken and confused. "She was wearing a long white gown," he told his wife, "and I know I hit her. It's like she just disappeared into thin air!"

This mysterious incident took place in 1987. More than forty other similar incidents have been reported over the years on this same highway. All drivers claimed to have hit a woman in white, but they could not find a body.

Not far from the scene of these "nonaccidents" is Samlesbury Hall, reportedly haunted by the ghost of Lady Dorothy Southworth. As the story goes, about four hundred years ago Lady Dorothy, a Roman Catholic, fell deeply in love with a Protestant boy. Because of their religious differences, the couple was forbidden by their families to see each other.

They continued to meet in secret, however, and one day made plans to elope. Unfortunately, Dorothy's brothers overheard the couple's plans. When her lover came to take her away, the brothers killed him and his companion, then secretly buried the bodies on the grounds of Samlesbury Hall.

When Lady Dorothy heard the news, she was heartbroken and died soon afterward from grief.

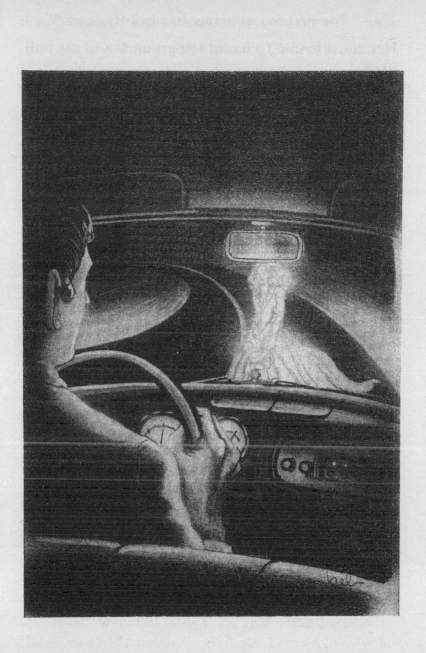

Her ghost is said to haunt the grounds and the hall itself.

In the early nineteenth century, the skeletons of two men were reportedly discovered near the hall. It is not certain whether these are the remains of Lady Dorothy's lover and his friend.

Over the years, people have reported seeing the ghost of Lady Dorothy, dressed all in white, and many have heard her crying. She has sometimes been seen walking among the trees outside the hall.

Drivers claim they have seen her by the side of the road. Some have stopped to offer her a ride, but when they approach her, she mysteriously disappears.

Is the strange apparition really the ghost of the heartbroken Lady Dorothy? Or could there be some other explanation as to why so many drivers have reported seeing a mysterious woman in white? Can these sightings be a mass hallucination or overactive imaginations at work? You be the judge.

Bridey Murphy

"Keep your eyes on the candle flame," said hypnotist Morey Bernstein to his subject, Ruth Simmons.

It was Saturday, November 29, 1952. Bernstein was attempting age-regression hypnosis. While the subject was in a hypnotic trance, he would take her back in time to when she was a youngster, and then farther back to when she was an infant.

In this particular attempt, Bernstein wanted to keep on going and try to take the woman back to the time *before* her birth to see if any memories existed.

"You will fall into a deeper and deeper sleep," Bernstein explained to his subject as she remained in a trance. "Now we are going to turn back time and space, and when I next talk to you, you will be seven years old, and you will answer my questions."

Ruth responded to questions first as a seven-year-old then as a five-year-old, a three-year-old, and a one-year-old.

"Now I want you to keep on going back and back in your mind," continued Bernstein. "Keep going back until you find yourself in some other scene at some other time. You will be able to talk to me about it and answer my questions."

After several minutes, Bernstein asked, "How old are you?"

"Eight," the subject replied.

"Now that you are eight years old, do you know what year it is?" the hypnotist asked softly.

"1806," she declared.

"What is your name?"

"Bridey . . . Bridey Murphy," answered the subject.

In a series of five interviews, all recorded on tape, Bernstein questioned his subject about nineteenth-century Ireland, where Bridey Murphy said she lived. Ruth had never been to Ireland, but as Bridey she revealed specific details of Irish life nearly a hundred years earlier.

According to Ruth, Bridey was born in 1798 and lived in the town of Cork. She was the daughter of Duncan and Kathleen Murphy. Bridey married

Brian McCarthy and moved to Belfast, where she died at age sixty-six in 1864.

The case of Bridey Murphy received much publicity in the 1950s. Bernstein wrote a best-selling book about it and the tape recordings of the hypnosis sessions were sold.

Many attempts were made to find out if Bridey Murphy really existed. Unfortunately, no birth or death records were kept that far back in Ireland.

During Bernstein's interviews, Bridey mentioned the names of two grocers in Belfast from whom she bought food. One was Mr. Farr and the other was John Carrigan. A Belfast librarian found a city directory for 1865–1866 that listed both men as grocers.

Does this prove reincarnation is real? Are people reborn after death into new lives? Have we all lived as different people in the past? Or did Ruth, under hypnosis, completely fantasize the character of Bridey Murphy?

Although many case details were found to be correct, some people believed that Ruth's memories as Bridey were actually taken from Ruth's own childhood remembrances. Ruth's aunt, Marie Burns, was Irish, but she grew up in New York, not Ireland. An Irishwoman named Bridey Corkell lived across the street from Marie and her husband. Did the details of Bridey Murphy's life, as well as her first name, come from this neighbor?

Many people have had experiences that they feel

they have been through before. The French call it *déjà vu*. Does *déjà vu* prove that reincarnation exists, or is it just a memory of a similar scene in our present life that has been forgotten?

There are no definite answers to the case of Bridey Murphy and the question of reincarnation. The search to solve the mystery continues. Is the end really a new beginning? No one knows for sure.

Flight to Nowhere

"James, I'm taking a Camel to Tadcaster Airfield," said Lieutenant David M'Connel to his friend, Lieutenant James Larkin. "I expect to be back in time for tea. Cheerio!"

Both young men were pilots stationed at Scampton Airfield in Lincolnshire, England. It was a December morning in 1918.

David planned to fly the sixty miles to Tadcaster to make a delivery in his Sopwith Camel biplane. He sat in an open cockpit behind twin machine guns, goggles over his eyes.

The Camel was a fragile airplane by today's standards. Its wings were made of wood and fabric. It stood only 8½ feet high and was less than 19 feet long!

James spent the afternoon writing letters and reading in front of the fire, waiting for David to return. At about 3:30 P.M., the door opened and David stepped into the room.

"Hello, old boy," he said to James, who turned to face his friend.

James saw David standing in the doorway, dressed in his flying clothes. His cap was pushed back on his head, and he was smiling.

"Hello. Back already?" asked James.

"Yes," David replied. "Got there all right and had a fine trip. Well, cheerio!" He turned and left.

David went on reading. About fifteen minutes later, a pilot friend came into the room and said, "I hope M'Connel gets back early. We're going to Lincoln this evening."

"But he *is* back," James declared. "He was here just a few minutes ago."

"I'll try and find him," said the pilot.

It wasn't until later that evening that James heard the awful news. David and another flyer had been caught in a thick blanket of fog on the way to the Tadcaster field. The other man made a forced landing, but David continued on, trying to get through the fog and stay at a safe altitude.

A short distance from Tadcaster, the Camel, which had a reputation as a difficult plane to fly, went into a nosedive. It crashed, and David was killed when his head struck one of the machine guns in front of the cockpit. His watch was recov-

ered from the wreckage. It had stopped at 3:25 P.M.

"That's almost precisely the time I saw David in the room," declared an astonished James.

"Perhaps you were mistaken about David and the time," said his pilot friend. "Maybe you dreamed the whole episode."

"I was definitely wide awake, and I know what time it was," insisted James. "David looked so normal and yet, I must have seen him at the exact moment of his death!"

In a letter to David's father, James wrote: "I am of such a skeptical nature regarding things of this kind that even now I wish to think otherwise—that I did not see him—but I am unable to do so."

Did James simply imagine the meeting with David? Or did he see the ghost of his friend, who had returned to talk with him just one last time?

What do *you* think?

Glossary

CLAIRVOYANCE: the ability to identify or become aware of an object, person, or event without using the five basic senses (sight, hearing, smell, taste, and touch).

COINCIDENCE: occurrences of events that seem related but are not actually connected.

CURATOR: the person in charge of a museum, zoo, library, or other exhibit.

DÉJÀ VU: the feeling that something has been experienced before.

DEMONOLOGIST: an expert on the supernatural and the spirit world.

DOWSING: to search for a water or mineral source using a special stick or rod.

ELECTROMAGNETIC: magnetism that is produced by
a current of electricity.

EXORCISM: a special ceremony used to cast out evil
spirits and demons.

EXTRASENSORY PERCEPTION (ESP): special abilities
and knowledge that extend beyond the normal
five senses.

FLINTLOCK: a seventeenth- or eighteenth-century
gun in which the powder is exploded by a spark
produced when a flint strikes a metal plate.

HALLUCINATION: seeing people or things that aren't
really there.

KNOTS: a ship's speed. A knot is one nautical mile
per hour.

LEVITATION: the lifting up or floating of a medium
or others at a séance.

MEDIUM: a person who communicates with the
dead.

PAYLOAD: the cargo of a vehicle.

PHENOMENA: extraordinary or unusual occurrences.

POLTERGEIST: a noisy or mischievous ghost that often moves objects from place to place.

PRECOGNITION: the knowledge of events before they actually happen.

PREMONITION: an advance warning of an event; similar to precognition.

PSYCHIC: a person who is sensitive to supernatural forces.

REINCARNATION: the belief that a person's soul is reborn in a new human body after death.

SCAVENGER: someone who collects or uses discarded or leftover objects.

SÉANCE: a sitting with a medium to contact otherworldly spirits.

SUPERNATURAL: anything caused by other than the known forces of nature.

Bibliography

Arvey, Michael. *Reincarnation*. San Diego, Calif.: Greenhaven Press, 1989.

Barrett, Sir William, and Theodore Besterman. *The Divining Rod*. New Hyde Park, N.Y.: University Books, 1968.

Bernstein, Morey. *The Search for Bridey Murphy*. Garden City, N.Y.: Doubleday, 1956.

Bro, Harmon Hartzell. *A Seer Out of Season: The Life of Edgar Cayce*. New York: New American Library, 1989.

Broughton, Richard S. *Parapsychology: The Controversial Science*. New York: Ballantine, 1991.

Brown, Raymond Lamont. *Phantoms of the Theater*. Nashville: Thomas Nelson, 1977.

Brown, Rosemary. *Unfinished Symphonies*. New York: William Morrow, 1971.

Cohen, Daniel. *Phone Call from a Ghost*. New York: G. P. Putnam's Sons, 1988.

Cohen, Daniel. *The Ghosts of War*. New York: G. P. Putnam's Sons, 1990.

Constable, George, ed. *Ghosts*. Alexandria, Virg.: Time-Life Books, 1984.

Constable, George, ed. *Psychic Powers*. Alexandria, Virg.: Time-Life Books, 1987.

Constable, George, ed. *Phantom Encounters*. Alexandria, Virg.: Time-Life Books, 1988.

Constable, George, ed. *Visions and Prophecies*. Alexandria, Virg.: Time-Life Books, 1988.

Curran, Robert. *The Haunted*. New York: St. Martin's Press, 1988.

Day, James Wentworth. *In Search of Ghosts*. New York: Taplinger, 1970.

Fairley, John, and Simon Welfare. *Arthur C. Clarke's World of Strange Powers*. New York: G. P. Putnam's Sons, 1984.

Gardner, Colin B., ed. *Ghostwatch*. London, England: Foulsham, 1989.

Gauld, Alan, and A. D. Cornell. *Poltergeists*. London, England: Routledge & Kegan Paul, 1979.

Halifax, Viscount Charles Lindley. *Lord Halifax's Ghost Book*. Secaucus, N.J.: Castle Books, 1986.

Hall, Trevor H. *New Light on Old Ghosts*. London, England: Gerald Duckworth & Co. Ltd., 1965.

Holzer, Hans. *Ghost Hunt*. Norfolk, Virg.: Donning Company Publishers, 1983.

Kettlekamp, Larry. *Mischievous Ghosts*. New York: William Morrow, 1980.

Knight, David C., ed. *The ESP Reader*. New York: Grosset & Dunlap, 1969.

MacManus, Diarmuid. *Between Two Worlds*. Gerrards Cross, Buckinghamshire, England: Colin Smythe Ltd., 1977.

Marsden, Simon. *The Haunted Realm*. New York: Dutton, 1986.

May, Antoinette. *Haunted Houses of California*. San Carlos, Calif.: Wide World Publishing/Tetra, 1990.

McHargue, Georgess. *Facts, Frauds, and Phantasms*. Garden City, N.Y.: Doubleday, 1972.

Myers, Arthur. *Ghosts of the Rich and Famous*. Chicago: Contemporary Books, 1988.

Prince, Walter Franklin. *Noted Witnesses for Psychic Occurrences*. New Hyde Park, N.Y.: University Books, 1928.

Reynolds, James. *Ghosts in Irish Houses*. New York: Bonanza Books, 1957.

Roberts, Nancy. *Haunted Houses*. Chester, Conn.: Globe Pequot Press, 1988.

Shoemaker, John Bruce, Ben Williams, and Jean Williams. *The Black Hope Horror*. New York: William Morrow, 1991.

Smith, Susy. *Haunted Houses for the Millions*. Los Angeles: Sherbourne Press, 1967.

Stemman, Roy. *Spirits and Spirit Worlds*. London, England: Danbury Press, 1975.

Stevens, Austin N. *Mysterious New England*. Dublin, N.H.: Yankee, 1971.

Tabori, Paul. *Harry Price: The Biography of a Ghost Hunter*. New York: Living Books, 1966.

Taylor, L. B. Jr. *Haunted Houses*. New York: Julian Messner, 1983.

Underwood, Peter. *A Gazetteer of Scottish and Irish Ghosts*. New York: Walker and Company, 1973.

Walker, Danton. *I Believe in Ghosts*. New York: Taplinger, 1969.

Warren, Ed and Lorraine, with Robert David Chase. *Ghost Hunters*. New York: St. Martin's Press, 1989.

Westbie, Constance, and Harold Cameron. *Night Stalks the Mansion*. Harrisburg, Penn.: Stackpole Books, 1978.

Wilson, Colin. *Poltergeist*. New York: G. P. Putnam's Sons, 1981.

Wylder, Joseph Edward. *Psychic Pets*. New York: Stonehill, 1978.